I Am Loved
Celebrating God's Incredible Love for You!

Bible text selections from the
International Children's Bible®
Copyright © 1986, 1988, 1999 by Thomas Nelson, Inc. All Rights Reserved.

General Editor: Sheila Walsh
Gigi, God's Little Princess™ illustrations copyright © 2005 by Sheila Walsh
Illustrator: Meredith Johnson
Published in association with the literary agency of Alive Communications, Inc.,
7680 Goddard Street, Suite 200, Colorado Springs, CO 80920. www.alivecommunications.com.

Published in Nashville, Tennessee, by Thomas Nelson, Inc.

Typeset, design and spot art by: Koechel Peterson & Associates, Inc., Minneapolis, MN
Editorial Team: Jennifer Morgan Gerelds, writer; Beverly Riggs, editor

DSC
Shenzhen, China
June, 2015
PPO # 9348448

Printed in China
5 6 7 8 9 – 18 17 16 15

God's Little Princess®

I Am Loved

Celebrating God's Incredible Love for You!

Sheila Walsh

International Children's Bible

A Division of Thomas Nelson Publishers

NASHVILLE   MEXICO CITY   RIO DE JANEIRO

Dear Princess,

I am so glad you are holding this book in your hands. It is filled with the very best news in the whole wide world: you are a Princess and God loves you so much! But let me ask you, do you ever have a day when you don't feel very special? Do you ever lay your head down on the pillow at night and wonder if you are really loved? You will discover in the pages of this book that God thinks you are such a special girl—so special that he calls you his Princess. His love for you is amazing and it never changes. Whether you are having a good day or a bad day, God loves you just the same. Perhaps you look at yourself in the mirror some days and you see some things you don't like. When God looks at you, he thinks you are beautiful all the time. There is no one else in the world quite like you.

You may wonder, well, how does a Princess behave? what does she do? This book is filled with lots of fun ideas and games to help you live the Princess life. More than anything, it is my prayer for you, Sweet Princess, that you would know deep in your heart that you are loved ... you are special ... you are treasured by God.

With love,
Your big sister,
Sheila

LIVIN' THE PRINCESS LIFE

Livin' the Princess Life:
Great articles to show you how
to live your life based on the
wisdom, promises, and truth from
the Bible and your King! Livin' your
life according to God's Word and his love for you will
help you be the best you can be!

Royal Connections

Royal Connections: Ever wonder
how to get along with others
or how to have strong bonds
with family and friends? Royal
Connections can help you learn
"tried and true" ways, through God's love
and compassion, to live happily with
the people in your life.

Faithful Love

Faithful Love: God shows his love
for us in many ways. Through the
evidence of his faithful love, God
proves just how much he cares!

Perfect Princess Praise

Perfect Princess Praise: Because God demonstrates his love throughout the Bible, little princesses can learn how to praise the giver of that love, God.

Precious Promises: God's incredible love is shown through the many promises he shares all the way through the Bible. Selected scriptures are highlighted to give girls the reassurance of God's promises just for them. Learn them all and "hide them in your heart."

Crafts and Recipes: Fun recipes you can make and eat, and simple crafts to do with your family—all related to Bible stories!

Table of Contents

Marvelous Masterpiece

GENESIS 1:26-31

God said, "Let us make human beings in our image and likeness. And let them rule over the fish in the sea and the birds in the sky. Let them rule over the tame animals, over all the earth and over all the small crawling animals on the earth."

So God created human beings in his image. In the image of God he created them. He created them male and female. God blessed them and said, "Have many children and grow in number. Fill the earth and be its master. Rule over the fish in the sea and over the birds in the sky. Rule over every living thing that moves on the earth."

4-20-16

God said, "Look, I have given you all the plants that have grain for seeds. And I have given you all the trees whose fruits have seeds in them. They will be food for you. I have given all the green plants to all the animals to eat. They will be food for every wild animal, every bird of the air and every small crawling animal." And it happened. God looked at everything he had made, and it was very good. Evening passed, and morning came. This was the sixth day.

LIVIN' THE PRINCESS LIFE

With a word he put the stars in place.
He spoke, and the world came to be.
Trees, birds, fish, mountains, oceans.
And at the center of it, in charge of it,
he made us—people created in his very
image. And do you know what God
said? He said, "It was very good."

So here you are, thousands of years
later. When you look in the mirror, what
do you see? Do you sometimes not like
what you see? Take a look again and see
with God's eyes. He still smiles at you.
You are his special creation. Because of
Christ, we are marvelous in his sight.

Enjoy being special and that you were made perfectly to fulfill God's very amazing plan for your life.

I know I am loved because...

...God made me in his image!

Sleep on It

GENESIS 2:2–7

By the seventh day God finished the work he had been doing. So on the seventh day he rested from all his work. God blessed the seventh day and made it a holy day. He made it holy because on that day he rested. He rested from all the work he had done in creating the world.

This is the story of the creation of the sky and the earth. When the Lord God made the earth and the sky, there were no plants on the earth. Nothing was growing in the fields. The Lord God had not yet made it rain on the land. And there was no

LIVIN' THE PRINCESS LIFE

man to care for the ground. But a mist often rose from the earth and watered all the ground.

Then the Lord God took dust from the ground and formed man from it. The Lord breathed the breath of life into the man's nose. And the man became a living person.

LIVIN' THE PRINCESS LIFE

Do you think creating the universe was tough stuff? Did God really need to take a break when it was all done? Did creation make him tired before it even got started?

No, the Bible says that God never sleeps. So why did he rest on the seventh day? He rested for us. He was creating a picture for us so we would follow in his footsteps. People do need rest. Being active is a good thing. But God also wants us to set aside time to focus on him. It's like a timeout to remember what and who is really important in life. It's a special blessing that God gives to his people to attend church services each week. This Sunday, ask God how he would like you to rest—and enjoy your day with him.

I know I am loved because...
...God created a day of rest for me to enjoy and worship him!

Not Always Fun

GENESIS 7:1, 4–5, 7–9

The Lord said to Noah, "I have seen that you are the best man among the people of this time. So you and your family go into the boat.... Seven days from now I will send rain on the earth. It will rain 40 days and 40 nights. I will destroy from the earth every living thing that I made."

Noah did everything that the Lord commanded him....

He and his wife and his sons and their wives went into the boat. They went in to escape the waters of the flood. The clean animals, the unclean animals, the birds and everything that crawls on the ground came to Noah. They went into the boat in groups of two, male and female. This was just as God had commanded Noah.

LIVIN' THE PRINCESS LIFE

Have you ever wondered how Noah must have felt when he heard the door of the boat (sometimes called an ark) close behind him? He knew his world was about to change forever. He knew that he was locked in a boat with some family and a whole lot of animals . . . and it probably wasn't going to be fun.

Sometimes obeying God may make you feel like you're getting on your own ark. You don't know where you are going. And it doesn't seem like much fun. But remember Noah and God when life gets you down. Though Noah didn't know what was going to happen, God did. We can't make our lives turn out the way we think they should. Instead, we must obey God and trust him to make life the way he wants it to be for us. He promises to use each moment for good in our lives. Even when it's not so fun, look to the sky and imagine God's rainbow of promise shining over you the whole time.

I know I am loved because...

...God sent the rainbow to always remind me!

Best Friends

When Abram was 99 years old, the Lord appeared to him. The Lord said, "I am God All-Powerful. Obey me and do what is right. I will make an agreement between us. I will make you the ancestor of many people."

Then Abram bowed facedown on the ground. God said to him, "I am making my agreement with you: I will make you the father of many nations. I am changing your name from Abram to Abraham. This is because I am making you a father of many nations. I will give you many descendants. New nations will be born from you. Kings will come from you. And I will make an agreement between me and you and all your descendants from now on: I will be your

14

God and the God of all your descendants."

Later, the Lord again appeared to Abraham near the great trees of Mamre. At that time Abraham was sitting at the door of his tent. It was during the hottest part of the day. He looked up and saw three men standing near him. When Abraham saw them, he ran from his tent to meet them. He bowed facedown on the ground before them. Abraham said, "Sir, if you think well of me, please stay awhile with me your servant. I will bring some water so all of you can wash your feet. You may rest under the tree. I will get some bread for you, so you can regain your strength. Then you may continue your journey."

15

Isn't it great how the Lord and Abraham just sat and talked? God showed up as a man. He talked with and even ate food with Abraham. God treated him as a close friend.

Do you ever wish that God still worked the same way today? It seems hard to have a real friendship with someone you can't see. But God has asked us to trust him. We don't have to see his face, because the Bible teaches us about how he loves us. As we believe what he says in the Bible, we understand that he is a part of every moment of our day. We don't have to say big prayers all the time. We can talk to him just like we would talk to our best friend. Let him know what you're thinking or what you need. And listen in your heart for him to answer. Like Abraham, you'll discover that you have the God of creation as your very best friend.

I know I am loved because . . .

. . . God is my always and forever best friend.

No Soup for You

One day Jacob was boiling a pot of vegetable soup. Esau came in from hunting in the fields. He was weak from hunger. So Esau said to Jacob, "Let me eat some of that red soup. I am weak with hunger."...

But Jacob said, "You must sell me your rights as the firstborn son."

Esau said, "I am almost dead from hunger. If I die, all of my father's wealth will not help me."

But Jacob said, "First, promise me that you will give it to me." So Esau made a promise to Jacob. In this way he sold his

part of their father's wealth to Jacob. Then Jacob gave Esau bread and vegetable soup. Esau ate and drank and then left. So Esau showed how little he cared about his rights as the firstborn son.

LIVIN' THE PRINCESS LIFE

Imagine if someone called you to say you had won a million dollars. Would you be excited, or would you not take the money and ask for a kids' fun meal instead? Believe it or not, Esau was actually guilty of passing up his right to a double portion of his father's riches because he chose some soup instead. He wanted to satisfy himself right away, instead of waiting for something much better.

As Christians, we need to understand that God has given us everything we need to live holy lives that please him.

Like Esau, sometimes we want to give up or give in. We want things right now and don't take time to thank God for what we already have. We need to thank God and ask him for strength to live every moment because we are God's children. Everything we do should be for his glory.

I know I am loved because...

...God gives me everything I need to live a life for him.

For Goodness Sake

oseph was born when his father Israel, also called Jacob, was old. So Israel loved Joseph more than his other sons. He made Joseph a special robe with long sleeves. Joseph's brothers saw that their father loved Joseph more than he loved them. So they hated their brother and could not speak to him politely....

Joseph had been taken down to Egypt. An Egyptian named Potiphar was an officer to the king of Egypt. He was the captain of the palace guard. He bought Joseph from

22

the Ishmaelites who had brought him down there. The Lord was with Joseph, and he became a successful man. He lived in the house of his master, Potiphar the Egyptian.

Potiphar saw that the Lord was with Joseph. He saw that the Lord made Joseph successful in everything he did. So Potiphar was very happy with Joseph. He allowed Joseph to be his personal servant. He put Joseph in charge of the house. Joseph was trusted with everything Potiphar owned.

It was much worse than just being teased. Joseph realized his brothers actually hated him so much they even thought about killing him. They were jealous of his special coat and their father's love for Joseph. Then they sold him for almost nothing to become a slave in a faraway land.

But after Joseph had endured years of hard times, and even ruled the Egyptian kingdom, he said to his brothers, "You meant it for evil, but God meant it for good." He wasn't bitter or angry. God gave Joseph the wisdom to see that no matter what people try to do to us, God is the one who still controls our every moment. Like Joseph, we need to remember God's goodness, and that he promises to make all things work for the best in our lives.

I know I am loved because . . .

. . . God is in control!

Love Our Leaders

The king said to Joseph, "…There is no one as wise and understanding as you are. I will put you in charge of my palace. All the people will obey your orders. Only I will be greater than you."

Then the king said to Joseph, "Look! I have put you in charge of all the land of Egypt."

Then the king took off from his own finger his ring with the royal seal on it. And he put it on Joseph's finger. He gave Joseph fine linen clothes to wear. And he put a gold chain around Joseph's neck. The king had Joseph ride in the second royal chariot. Men walked ahead of his

chariot calling, "Bow down!" By doing these things the king put Joseph in charge of all of Egypt.

The king said to him, "I am the king. And I say that no one in all the land of Egypt may lift a hand or a foot unless you say he may." The king gave Joseph the name Zaphenath-Paneah. He also gave Joseph a wife name Asenath. She was the daughter of Potiphera, priest of On. So Joseph traveled through all the land of Egypt.

Joseph was 30 years old when he began serving the king of Egypt. And he left the king's court and traveled through all the land of Egypt.

Royal Connections

While good things do happen in the world, there are many bad things that happen, too. War, famine, earthquakes, crime, poverty, and countless other problems are things people deal with every day.

Sometimes life can be hard. But God has given us leaders to help us. Our police, government, and soldiers are all people that help keep the peace here at home. Their jobs are not easy, and they cannot do it alone. We can help them, though, by obeying the rules they give

us. And we can pray for them every day. Through our prayers God can bring us peace.

I know I am loved because . . .

. . . God gives me leaders to protect me.

Sister Smarts

There was a man from the family of Levi. He married a woman who was also from the family of Levi. She became pregnant and gave birth to a son. She saw how wonderful the baby was, and she hid him for three months. But after three months, she was not able to hide the baby any longer. So she got a basket made of reeds and covered it with tar so that it would float. She put the baby in the basket. Then she put the basket among the tall grass at the edge of the Nile River. The baby's sister stood a short distance away. She wanted to see what would happen to him.

Then the daughter of the king of Egypt came to the river. She was going to take a bath. Her servant girls were walking beside the river. She saw the basket in the tall grass. So she sent her slave girl to get it. The king's daughter opened the basket and saw the baby boy. He was crying, and she felt sorry for him. She said, "This is one of the Hebrew babies."

Then the baby's sister asked the king's daughter, "Would you like me to find a Hebrew woman to nurse the baby for you?"

The king's daughter said, "Yes, please." So the girl went and got the baby's own mother.

LIVIN' THE PRINCESS LIFE

Terrible times had come upon the Hebrew people. All their baby boys were being killed by the Egyptians who ruled over them. So what did Moses' mom do? She put him in a basket and sent him floating down the Nile River.

That could have been the end of the story. But Moses' sister Miriam followed closely and watched the king's daughter. The Egyptian princess found—and

kept—baby Moses as her own. Miriam offered to find a Hebrew woman to nurse the baby. Moses' very own mother took care of him right under the protection of the king himself!

Moses' sister found a way to reconnect her mom and baby Moses together. Like her, we can connect people with God's love. Don't be afraid because you're young. Look for the right moment, and share God with them.

I know I am loved because...

...God can help me tell others about him.

Super Support

M oses said to the Lord, "But Lord, I am not a skilled speaker. I have never been able to speak well. And now, even after talking to you, I am not a good speaker. I speak slowly and can't find the best words."

Then the Lord said to him, "Who made man's mouth? And who makes him deaf or not able to speak? Or who gives a man sight or makes him blind? It is I, the Lord. Now go! I will help you speak. I will tell you what to say."

But Moses said, "Please, Lord, send someone else."

The Lord became angry with Moses. He said, "Your brother Aaron, from the family of Levi, is a skilled speaker. He is already coming to meet you. And he will be happy when he sees you. I will tell you what to say. Then you will tell Aaron. I will help both of you know what to say and do."

Moses had all the training he needed. But he was still afraid to go talk to Pharaoh and ask him to set the Israelites free. Though God could have easily forced him, he instead gave Moses a strong brother to help him.

Life is easier with friends. And obeying God is easier when we are surrounded by other people who want to obey God, too. The Bible says that two are better than one because they can help each other.

What about you? Do you have friends or family who can help you know God better? Pray that God will bring great friends to you. Also pray that you can be a special friend to them.

I know I am loved because . . .

. . . God sends friends to help us in life!

Hidden Danger

NUMBERS 22:21-28

Balaam ... put a saddle on his donkey. Then he went with the Moabite leaders. But God became angry because Balaam went. So the angel of the Lord stood in the road to stop Balaam. Balaam was riding his donkey. And he had two servants with him. The donkey saw the angel of the Lord standing in the road. The angel had a sword in his hand. So the donkey left the road and went into the field. Balaam hit the donkey to force her back on the road.

Later, the angel of the Lord stood on a narrow path between two vineyards. There were walls on both sides. Again the donkey

saw the angel of the Lord. So the donkey walked close to one wall. This crushed Balaam's foot against the wall. So he hit her again.

The angel of the Lord went ahead again. The angel stood at a narrow place. It was too narrow to turn left or right. The donkey saw the angel of the Lord. So she lay down under Balaam. Balaam was very angry and hit her with his stick. Then the Lord made the donkey talk.

Royal Connections

Balaam couldn't believe it. Whack after whack, and still his faithful donkey stood still. It wasn't until the donkey spoke out loud, and Balaam's eyes were opened to see the angel in front of him, that Balaam understood.

We know that our parents are supposed to discipline us. But when we are going through it, it is often hard to take. We may think, *What are they doing?* or *Why don't they let me do what I want?* Just like Balaam, as kids we often don't—and can't—see the big picture. But our parents can. When they correct us or keep us from doing something we want to do, we shouldn't have bad attitudes or misbehave. We should trust that they have our best interests at heart (like Balaam's faithful donkey). Thank God that he protects you through your parents.

I know I am loved because . . .

. . . of my parents' love and protection for me.

Boom! It Fell Down

On the seventh day they got up at dawn. They marched around the city seven times. They marched just as they had on the days before. But on that day they marched around the city seven times. The seventh time around the priests blew their trumpets. Then Joshua gave the command: "Now, shout! The Lord has given you this city! The city and everything in it are to be destroyed as an offering to the Lord.... Don't take any of the things that are to be destroyed as an offering to the Lord. If you take them and bring them into our camp, then you yourselves will be

destroyed. You will also bring trouble to all Israel. All the silver and gold and things made from bronze and iron belong to the Lord. They must be saved for him."

When the priests blew the trumpets, the people shouted. At the sound of the trumpets and the people's shout, the walls fell. And everyone ran straight into the city. So the Israelites defeated that city.

43

LIVIN' THE PRINCESS LIFE

Can't you imagine how Joshua must have felt when God told him how he planned to conquer Jericho? Without a weapon, the Israelites simply marched one time around the city, six days in a row. Then on the seventh day, they marched around it seven times, and BOOM! Down went the walls, and Jericho belonged to Israel.

One of the biggest things you'll learn about God when you hear the Old Testament stories is that he does not do things we would consider "normal." He has his own special ways of doing things. Sometimes we can't understand them. That's why faith is so important. We must trust in his goodness and that he knows what he's doing, even if it seems a little silly to us. God will do amazing things in incredible ways through our lives, too, if we will listen to him and trust him.

I know I am loved because . . .

. . . God does incredible things for me!

A Sticky Situation

RUTH 1:11–17

Naomi said, "My daughters, go back to your own homes. Why do you want to go with me? I cannot give birth to more sons to give you new husbands. So go back to your own homes. I am too old to have another husband. But even if I had another husband tonight and if I had more sons, it wouldn't help! Would you wait until the babies were grown into men? Would you live for so many years without husbands? Don't do this thing. My life is much too sad for you to share. This is because the Lord is against me!"

The women cried together again. Then Orpah kissed Naomi good-bye, but Ruth held on to her.

Naomi said, "Look, your sister-in-law is going back to her own people and her own gods. Go back with her."

Ruth said, "Don't ask me to leave you! Don't beg me not to follow you! Every place you go, I will go. Every place you live, I will live. Your people will be my people. Your God will be my God. And where you  die, I will die. And there I will be buried. I ask the Lord to punish me terribly if I do not keep this promise: Only death will separate us."

LIVIN' THE PRINCESS LIFE

Naomi's husband and two sons had died. Ruth was Naomi's daughter-in-law. Normally, Ruth would have returned to her homeland of Moab after her husband died. But she didn't. She stayed with Naomi and promised to be with her no matter what. Naomi loved the one true God. Ruth had come to know and love the same God. She was willing to give up the life she had known to follow what she learned to be the truth.

In the end, Ruth was rewarded for her obedience. God gave her a husband and made her part of the royal line of Christ. Like Ruth, we need to learn what is true and right and follow the Lord wherever he leads us. Following God always leads to blessing.

I know I am loved because . . .

. . . God shows me what is true and right!

More Than Skin Deep

1 SAMUEL 16:6-7, 12-13

Samuel saw Eliab. Samuel thought, "Surely the Lord has appointed this person standing here before him."

But the Lord said to Samuel, "Don't look at how handsome Eliab is. Don't look at how tall he is. I have not chosen him. God does not see the same way people see. People look at the outside of a person, but the Lord looks at the heart."...

So Jesse sent and had his youngest son brought in. He was a fine boy, tanned and handsome.

The Lord said to Samuel, "Go! Appoint him. He is the one."

LIVIN' THE PRINCESS LIFE

So Samuel took the container of olive oil. Then he poured oil on Jesse's youngest son to appoint him in front of his brothers. From that day on, the Lord's Spirit entered David with power.

The time had come to crown a new king. Samuel was clueless about God's choice. Samuel thought the biggest and best-looking boy should be chosen. But God thought differently and he chose David.

God is not concerned about how we look on the outside. After all, beauty on the outside doesn't last long at all. What God does care about is the character inside our hearts. He says that humble, obedient hearts are truly beautiful. Even though David wasn't the biggest or old-est, he was chosen as king because he loved God. Next time you look in the mirror remember David's story. Ask God to make your heart as beautiful as his.

I know I am loved because...
...God makes my heart beautiful.

Small Wonders

The Israelites and Philistines were lining up their men to face each other in battle.

David . . . ran to the battle line and talked to his brothers. While he was talking with them, Goliath came out. He was the Philistine champion from Gath. He shouted things against Israel as usual, and David heard it. When the Israelites saw Goliath, they were very much afraid and ran away. . . .

David asked the men who stood near him, "What will be done to reward the man who kills this Philistine? What will be done for whoever takes away the shame from Israel? Goliath is a Philistine. . . .

Why does he think he can speak against the armies of the living God?"...

David said to Saul, "Don't let anyone be discouraged. I, your servant, will go and fight this Philistine!"

LIVIN' THE PRINCESS LIFE

His brothers tried to send him away. They thought their younger brother was just getting in the way. But what they thought didn't matter to David. What the king thought didn't matter either. Even though he was only a young boy, David knew it was wrong for Goliath to make fun of God. So he did something about it.

You might think that you are too young to do anything for the Lord. Maybe you think it's something you can do someday when you are older. But God wants your attention right

now. It doesn't matter how young you are. What matters is that you belong to God. When you obey him, he gives you strength from heaven to do all the amazing works he has asked you to do.

I know I am loved because . . .

. . . God has a plan for my life!

Reaching Out

2 SAMUEL 9:3-7

The king asked, "Is there anyone left in Saul's family? I want to show God's kindness to this person."

Ziba answered the king, "Jonathan has a son still living. He is crippled in both feet."

The king asked Ziba, "Where is this son?"

Ziba answered, "He is at the house of Makir son of Ammiel in Lo Debar."

Then King David had servants bring Jonathan's son from the house of Makir son of Ammiel in Lo Debar. Mephibosheth,

Jonathan's son, came before David and bowed facedown on the floor.

David said, "Mephibosheth!"

Mephibosheth said, "I am your servant."

David said to him, "Don't be afraid. I will be kind to you for your father Jonathan's sake. I will give you back all the land of your grandfather Saul. And you will always be able to eat at my table."

59

Royal Connections

Even though David was king and had lots of kingly duties on his mind, he still did not forget the promise to his friend Jonathan. He looked hard to find Mephibosheth, Jonathan's crippled son. He brought him to his own palace to take care of him.

Do you know someone who has a disability—maybe a friend at school or church? Don't be afraid of them. Instead, show them Jesus' love by becoming their friend and helping them. As we take time to help others, we get a better understanding of how much God loves

us and how much he gives to us.
We also bring glory and
honor to God when we
treat others with love
and respect, the way
he treats us.

I know I am loved because...
...God helps me to serve and
care for others.

The Real Genie

1 KINGS 3:5–9

While [King Solomon] was at Gibeon, the Lord came to him in a dream during the night. God said, "Ask for anything you want. I will give it to you."

Solomon answered, "You were very kind to your servant, my father David. He obeyed you. He was honest and lived right. And you showed great kindness to him when you allowed his son to be king after him. Lord my God, you have allowed me to be king in my father's place. But I am like a little child. I do not have the wisdom I need to do what I must do. I, your servant, am here among your chosen people.

There are too many of them to count. So I ask that you give me wisdom. Then I can rule the people in the right way. Then I will know the difference between right and wrong. Without wisdom, it is impossible to rule this great people of yours."

LIVIN' THE PRINCESS LIFE

Have you ever seen Aladdin? In the story, a young Arab boy discovers a bottle. When he rubs it, a genie pops out and promises to grant whatever the boy wishes.

What would you wish?

In a way, a similar thing happened to Solomon. In a dream, God offered to grant whatever wish he had. But instead of asking for fame or money, Solomon wanted wisdom. God was more than happy to make Solomon the wisest man in the world.

Do you want to be wise like Solomon? We don't have to wait for a genie to pop out of a bottle. God promises to give us wisdom whenever we ask him for it. Remember that God values wisdom because it helps us know him better. As you go through your day, remember to ask God for wisdom to make the right decisions that honor him.

I know I am loved because...

...God gives me wisdom, especially when I pray.

What a Ride!

2 KINGS 2:1–3, 11–12

It was near the time for the Lord to take Elijah. He was going to take him by a whirlwind up into heaven. Elijah and Elisha were at Gilgal. Elijah said to Elisha, "Please stay here. The Lord has told me to go to Bethel."

But Elisha said, "As the Lord lives, and as you live, I won't leave you." So they went down to Bethel. A group of the prophets at Bethel came to Elisha. They said to him, "Do you know the Lord will take your master away from you today?"

Elisha said, "Yes, I know. But don't talk about it." . . .

Elijah and Elisha were still walking and talking. Then a chariot and horses of fire

separated Elijah from Elisha. Then Elijah went up to heaven in a whirlwind. Elisha saw it and shouted, "My father! My father! The chariots of Israel and their horsemen!" Elisha did not see him anymore. Elisha grabbed his own clothes and tore them to show how sad he was.

Elisha knew the time had come. All the prophets were saying it. God was about to take Elijah to heaven. But Elisha was so sad he didn't even want to talk about it.

Have you ever lost a loved one? We are almost never ready for the people we love to die, even if we know they are going to heaven. The loss just hurts our hearts, and God knows all about it. But the truth is, we all do have a time when our work on earth will be done. We won't get picked up in a fiery chariot

like Elijah did. But all those who belong
to Jesus will just as certainly one day
leave this world to be with Jesus in
heaven.

It's okay to be sad when someone dies,
but we should not lose hope. Remember
Jesus and the promise of being with him
in heaven when we accept his love.

I know I am loved because . . .
. . . of Jesus' love and salvation.

Fight for Families

2 KINGS 24:1-3, 5-6

While Jehoiakim was king, Nebuchadnezzar king of Babylon attacked the land of Judah. So Jehoiakim became Nebuchadnezzar's servant for three years. Then Jehoiakim turned against Nebuchadnezzar. And he broke away from his rule. The Lord sent men from Babylon, Aram, Moab and Ammon against Jehoiakim. He sent them to destroy Judah. This happened the way the Lord had said it would through his servants the prophets.

The Lord commanded this to happen to the people of Judah. He did it to remove them from his presence. This was because of all the sins Manasseh had done....

Royal Connections

The other things that happened while Jehoiakim was king and all he did are written down. They are in the book of the history of the kings of Judah. Jehoiakim died, and his son Jehoiachin became king in his place.

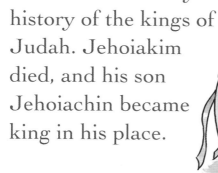

Royal Connections

Do you know kids whose parents have divorced? That is so sad, and they need our prayers. Do you know families with kids who don't obey or respect their parents? Even families that seemed strong at the beginning can begin to fall apart. Why?

Just like the children of Israel, we can forget about God. If we stop obeying and forget to read and listen to his Word, we can soon forget the truth. Forgetting God can tear families apart.

God wants us to stay strong as individuals and families. Pray right now that God would protect your parents and family. Ask for wisdom to help you make right choices and love each other.

I know I am loved because...

...God teaches me to love
my family and pray for them.

The Great Adventure

Esther's message was given to Mordecai. Then Mordecai gave orders to say to Esther: "Just because you live in the king's palace, don't think that out of all the Jews you alone will escape. You might keep quiet at this time. Then someone else will help and save the Jews. But you and your father's family will all die. And who knows, you may have been chosen queen for just such a time as this."

Then Esther sent this answer to Mordecai: "Go and get all the Jews in Susa together. For my sake, give up eating. Do not eat or

drink for three days, night and day. I and my
servant girls will also give up eating. Then I
will go to the king, even though it is against
the law. And if I die, I die."

So Mordecai went away.
He did everything Esther
had told him to do.

LIVIN' THE PRINCESS LIFE

Esther's life was an amazing, adventurous story! First, Esther's parents had died. She was an orphan until her cousin Mordecai adopted her as his own. Both she and Mordecai had been made prisoners under King Nebuchadnezzar's rule. Then, over all the other women in the kingdom, Esther was chosen to become the queen of Persia. As queen, she was able to save her people and defeat her enemies.

Sometimes we think we know how we want our lives to go. But God is the

one who plans our lives. He has incredible ideas for us beyond our wildest imaginations. We need to trust and rely on God's wisdom for our lives. Experiencing God's adventure is the only way to really live!

I know I am loved because...

...of God's amazing plan for my life!

The Believer's Bodyguard

PSALMS 3:3-5; 91:1-2, 9-11

ord, you are my shield.
You are my wonderful God who
gives me courage.
I will pray to the Lord.
And he will answer me from his
holy mountain.
I can lie down and go to sleep.
And I will wake up again
because the Lord protects me....
Those who go to God Most High
for safety
will be protected by God
All-Powerful.

Precious Promises

I will say to the Lord, "You are my place
of safety and protection.
You are my God, and I trust you."…
The Lord is your protection.
You have made God Most High your
place of safety.
Nothing bad will happen to you.
No disaster will come to your home.
He has put his angels in charge of you.
They will watch over you wherever
you go.

Precious Promises

If you think the President of the United States has a good secret service protection system, just take a look at what you have!

The Bible is packed full of verses that remind us over and over again that God himself watches his people and takes care of them. As if that weren't enough, God also gives each of his children their own secret service agents—angels! God says that real angels we cannot see are actually guarding, protecting, and comforting us.

Next time you are afraid, remember that God is always with you. His angels are all around you. So never fear! You couldn't be in safer hands.

I know I am loved because...

...God protects me!

Starry-Eyed

Lord our Master,
  your name is the most wonderful
    name in all the earth.
  It brings you praise in heaven above.
You have taught children and babies
  to sing praises to you. . . .
I look at the heavens,
  which you made with your hands.
I see the moon and stars,
  which you created.
But why is man important to you?
  Why do you take care of
    human beings?
You made man a little lower than
  the angels.

And you crowned him with glory
　　and honor.
You put him in charge of everything
　　you made.
　　You put all things under his control:
all the sheep, the cattle
　　and the wild animals,
the birds in the sky,
　　the fish in the sea,
　　and everything that lives
　　　under water.
Lord our Master,
　　your name is the most wonderful
　　　name in all the earth!

Perfect Princess Praise

Ever seen the sky on a clear night, away from city lights? Thousands of stars twinkle in view and fill your mind with God's incredible bigness.

David loved to stargaze, too. It would remind him — as it does us — of just how small we really are compared to the huge universe. But even though we're small, God sees us and loves us. He is aware of every thought we have, every word we say — he even knows the number of hairs on our heads! He says we are more important than all creation. Praise him now for noticing you and keeping you close to him always.

I know I am loved because . . .

. . . even though I'm small,
God knows all about me!

God Isn't Hiding

PSALMS 12:1–2, 7–8; 13:1–6

 ave me, Lord, because the good
people are all gone.
No true believers are left on earth.
Everyone lies to his neighbors.
They say one thing and mean
another. . . .
Lord, keep us safe.
Always protect us from such people.
The wicked are all around us.
Everyone loves what is wrong.
How long will you forget me, Lord?
How long will you hide from me?
Forever?
How long must I worry?
How long must I feel sad in
my heart?

Faithful Love

How long will my enemy win
over me?
Lord, look at me.
Answer me, my God.
Tell me, or I will die.
Otherwise my enemy will say,
"I have won!"
Those against me will rejoice that
I've been defeated.
I trust in your love.
My heart is happy because you
saved me.
I sing to the Lord
because he has taken care of me.

Faithful Love

David, who wrote these Psalms, was worried about his enemies. Even though he knew in his head that God was his friend, he felt very alone and afraid.

We often feel just like David did, too. Hard things happen, and God seems farther away than ever. David reminds us that even though we may feel left behind, God never leaves our side. Though we can't see or feel God's hand, we need to trust his promise of protection. As we learn to believe God in spite

of our feelings, our faith and confidence grow even stronger.

I know I am loved because...

...God is protecting me!

All I Need

PSALM 16:5-11

The Lord is all I need.
He takes care of me.
My share in life has been pleasant.
My part has been beautiful.
I praise the Lord because he guides me.
Even at night, I feel his leading.
I keep the Lord before me always.
Because he is close by my side
I will not be hurt.
So I rejoice, and I am glad.
Even my body has hope.

This is because you will not leave me
in the grave.
You will not let your holy one rot.
You will teach me God's way to live.
Being with you will fill me with joy.
At your right hand I will find
pleasure forever.

Faithful Love

Faithful Love

In our country, it is often hard to know the difference between what we need and what we want. Many things compete for our attention and affection. But Jesus says only one thing is really needed.

David knew what it was and wrote about it in Psalm 16. More than anything else in the world, we need to learn to make the Lord Jesus our friend. He is the one who gives our lives meaning. He protects us, guides us, loves us, and makes life beautiful. Without Jesus life means nothing. With him we have everything we need for this life and the next.

Tell Jesus today how grateful you are
for his everlasting friendship.

I know I am loved because...

...Jesus is my forever friend!

A Light in the Darkness

he Lord spared me because I did
what was right.
Because I have not done evil, he has
rewarded me.
I have followed the ways of the Lord.
I have not done evil by turning away
from my God.
I remember all his laws.
I have not broken his rules.
I am innocent before him.
I have kept myself from doing evil.
The Lord rewarded me because I did what
was right.
I did what the Lord said was right.

Faithful Love

Lord, you are loyal to those who
        are loyal.
    You are good to those who are good.
You are pure to those who are pure.
    But you are against those who
        are bad.
You save those who are not proud.
    But you make humble those who
        are proud.
Lord, you give light to my lamp.
    My God brightens the darkness
        around me.
With your help I can attack an army.
    With God's help I can jump over
        a wall.

Faithful Love

Did you know that you are a light? If you have God's Spirit inside you, the Bible says you have a hope that shines like a ray of light for others to see.

Look around you. Kids really want love, guidance, and meaning. Even adults seem worried and troubled some-times about things they cannot control.

But they are lost in the dark without the Lord. They need you to share with them the light of hope you have in Jesus. Tell them what Jesus did on the cross. Let them know that Jesus stands ready to forgive and to save. Invite them into the light of Jesus' love.

I know I am loved because...

...Jesus and his love are given to me to share!

Coming Attractions

PSALM 22:9–11, 14–15

You had my mother give birth to me.
You made me trust you
while I was just a baby.
I have leaned on you since the day I
was born.
You have been my God since my
mother gave birth to me.
So don't be far away from me.
Now trouble is near,
and there is no one to help....
My strength is gone
like water poured out onto the
ground.

All my bones are out of joint.
My heart is like wax.
    It has melted inside me.
My strength has dried up like a piece
        of a broken pot.
    My tongue sticks to the top
        of my mouth.
    You laid me in the dust of death.

Precious Promises

Didn't David live hundreds of years before Christ ever came? Then how can so many of his psalms describe Jesus so well?

God planned it that way. Ever since Adam and Eve made their big mistake in the garden, God promised to send a Savior who would help set things right. Many Old Testament passages tell us about it. Some places in Psalms, Isaiah, and other books tell about the coming Christ in ways such as his birth, his ministry, and even how he suffered on the cross. In God's time Jesus did come to earth, making all the Old Testament prophecies and God's promise of a Savior come true. Thank God today for his incredible plan of salvation!

I know I am loved because...
...God sent Jesus, his Son, to us!

The Flock's Focus

The Lord is my shepherd.
I have everything I need.
He gives me rest in green
        pastures.
    He leads me to calm water.
He gives me new strength.
For the good of his name,
    he leads me on paths that are right.
Even if I walk
    through a very dark valley,
I will not be afraid
    because you are with me.
Your rod and your shepherd's staff
        comfort me....

Shout to the Lord, all the earth.
Serve the Lord with joy.
Come before him with singing.
Know that the Lord is God.
He made us, and we belong to him.
We are his people, the sheep he tends.

Precious Promises

There are all kinds of kids in the world. Short ones, tall ones, smart, funny, rich, poor, thin, round, shy, bold, fast, and slow. All are unique and special, even when we sometimes don't think so!

If you belong to Jesus, you are God's kid. God himself tells you who you are, and he is always right. You are wonderful because God made you. That's why God's Word reminds us to keep our eyes on him. He is the Shepherd with the plan. We are like the sheep who trust his love and direction. Believe God's promise to guide you, feed you, and help you grow into the person he created you to be!

I know I am loved because...
...I am God's special child!

The Great Invitation

PSALM 25:8-14

The Lord is good and right.
He points sinners to the right way.
He shows those who are not proud how to
do right.
He teaches them his ways.
All the Lord's ways are loving and true
for those who follow the demands of
his agreement.
For the sake of your name, Lord,
forgive my many sins.
Is there someone who worships the Lord?
The Lord will point him to the best
way.

He will enjoy a good life.
His children will inherit the land.
The Lord tells his secrets to those who
respect him.
He tells them about his agreement.

Special Invitation

Precious Promises

Finally, they pick you. At last, you're a part of the team and in on the action.

It's a great feeling to be chosen, isn't it? Perhaps that's why God invites us to be a part of his team. He has plans he wants us to know. He wants us to know him like a friend so he can share his love with us. The greatest news of all is that he promises to guide us and help us make right choices. He wants us to listen to him and respect what he says. If we want to know God as much as possible, we must seek him with our whole heart. Ask him today to help you listen to his Spirit within you.

I know I am loved because ...

... God chose me!

Divine Design

he sky was made at the Lord's
command.
By the breath from his mouth,
he made all the stars.
He gathered the water in the sea into
a heap.
He made the great ocean stay in
its place.
All the earth should worship the Lord.
The whole world should fear him.
He spoke, and it happened.
He commanded, and it appeared.
The Lord upsets the plans of nations.
He ruins all their plans.
But the Lord's plans will stand forever.
His ideas will last from now on.

Happy is the nation whose God is the
Lord.
Happy are the people he chose for
his very own.
The Lord looks down from heaven.
He sees every person.
From his throne he watches
everyone who lives on earth.
He made their hearts.
He understands
everything
they do.

Perfect Princess Praise

Some scientists want us to believe that life is an accident. Somehow, they say, all the cells got together in just the right way to make insects, birds, trees, animals, and even people.

Is that the story you see when you look at nature? We see an incredible design that comes from God, the biggest and best Designer! How can a beautiful masterpiece happen without an artist? God's world silently shouts the truth. The mountains, seas, and everything in between declare the wisdom, love, and beauty of their Creator. He

made it for us to enjoy. He made it so we could see him in it. Every time you marvel at God's miraculous creation, give him praise for his creativity and power.

Let them praise his name in dance

I know I am loved because...

...God created this beautiful world for me to enjoy!

The Color of Joy

ord, your love reaches to the
heavens.
Your loyalty goes to the skies.
Your goodness is as high as the mountains.
Your justice is as deep as the great
ocean.
Lord, you protect both men and animals.
God, your love is so precious!
You protect people as a bird protects
her young under her wings.
They eat the rich food in your house.
You let them drink from your river
of pleasure.

You are the giver of life.
Your light lets us enjoy life.
Continue to love those who know you.
And continue to do good to those
who are good.

LIVIN' THE PRINCESS LIFE

What makes life fun? Why do we enjoy fun things like walks on the beach, time with friends, baking cookies, and more? God could have made life always very serious, plain, or boring. But he didn't. If we'll pay attention, we will see that life can be wonderful, colorful, exciting, and fun.

What makes life fun? The Bible says that it is the light of God that brings us joy. When we are really close to God, his light shines into every moment of our lives. We can see the smile of our

Creator peeking through as we enjoy the very thing he created us to enjoy. We can enjoy God as the giver of life. Thank him for the goodness and joy that come from every moment spent with him.

I know I am loved because . . .

. . . of the moments I spend with God.

Shout It Out

appy is the person
   who trusts the Lord.
He doesn't turn to those who are proud,
   to those who worship false gods.
Lord our God, you have done many
      miracles.
   Your plans for us are many.
If I tried to tell them all,
   there would be too many to count....
I will tell about your goodness in the
      great meeting of your people.
   Lord, you know my lips are not
      silent.
I do not hide your goodness in my heart.
   I speak about your loyalty and
      salvation.

118

I do not hide your love and truth
from the people in the great meeting.
Lord, do not hold back your mercy
from me.
Let your love and truth always
protect me.

Perfect Princess Praise

Are you shy? Are you afraid to share the story of God's love with others? If so, remember to keep your eyes on Jesus. Think about how wonderful God has been to you. Remember all the things God has given to you with your family, your home, your friends, and so much more.

As you remember, make it a point to share with others what you've learned. Tell them how God is a wonderful part of your life. When you talk about God's goodness, others will want to know him. We are actually worshiping God when we share what we know about him with our friends, family, and people we meet!

I know I am loved because...
...God helps me not to be afraid to tell others about him!

The Gift of Worry

God, listen to my prayer.
Do not ignore my prayer.
Pay attention to me and answer me.
I am troubled and upset.
by what the enemy says
and how the wicked look at me.
They bring troubles down on me.
In anger they attack me.
I am frightened inside.
The terror of death has attacked me.
I am scared and shaking.
Terror grips me.
I said, "I wish I had wings like a dove.
Then I would fly away and rest.
I would wander far away.
I would stay in the desert.

I would hurry to my place of escape,
  Far away from the wind and storm."...
But I will call to God for help.
  And the Lord will save me.
Morning, noon and night I am
    troubled and upset.
  But he will listen
    to me....
Give your worries to
    the Lord.
  He will take care
    of you.
He will never let good
    people down.

Precious Promises

What scares you? Sometimes life can be frightening, even more than roller coasters or scary movies. We fear losing our parents or our friends. We are afraid of what others might think of us. We are afraid to try something new. Maybe just being different from everybody else seems scary.

God says that we have something he wants us to give to him: He wants us to give him all of our worries. Whatever scares you in this life you should just give to God and let him take care of it.

He is stronger and more powerful than your greatest fear. He even promises to give you a peaceful heart and mind when you give your worries to him.

I know I am loved because...

...God does not want me to worry or be afraid!

Miraculous Moments

PSALM 65:8–13

 ven those people at the ends of the
earth fear your miracles.
You are praised from where the sun
rises to where it sets.
You take care of the land and water it.
You make it very fertile.
The rivers of God are full of water.
Grain grows because you make
it grow.
You cause rain to fall on the plowed fields.
You soak them with water.
You soften the ground with rain.
And then you bless it.

You give the year a good harvest.
You load the wagons with many
crops.
The desert is covered with grass.
The hills are covered with happiness.
The pastures are full of sheep.
The valleys are covered with grain.
Everything shouts and sings for joy.

Perfect Princess Praise

God did some amazing things in Old Testament times. He parted the Red Sea. He brought bread from heaven to his people in the wilderness. He made the sun stand still for a day! But what about now?

Miracles are not just part of the past. Every single moment in life is full of God's power. From each breath you take to every event that happens is all a gift from him to bring you closer to his heart. Think about all the ways you have seen God blessing you in your life.

Try to remember one good thing he has done for you each day. Offer him a prayer of thanks for all his miraculous ways!

I know I am loved because . . .

. . . he blesses me each day with every breath I take.

A Joyful Noise

Everything on earth, shout with joy
    to God!
Sing about his glory!
    Make his praise glorious!
Say to God, "Your works are amazing!
    Your power is great.
    Your enemies fall before you.
All the earth worships you.
    They sing praises to you.
    They sing praises to your name."
Come and see what God has done.
    See what amazing things he has done
        for people.

He turned the sea into dry land.
> The people crossed the river on foot.
> So let us rejoice because of what
>> he did.

He rules forever with his power.
> He keeps his eye on the nations.
> So people should not turn against
>> him.

You people, praise our God.
> Loudly sing his praise.

He protects our lives
> and does not let us be defeated.

God, you have tested us.
> You have purified us like silver.

LIVIN' THE PRINCESS LIFE

Even when he was busy out in the fields tending his sheep, David was always praising the Lord with his songs. David's harp often soothed King Saul's terrible temper when David played for him in his courts.

God has given us the gift of music, too. Even if we can't sing very well, we can make what David called "a joyful noise" to God. It just requires a grateful heart that longs to tell God how wonderful he is. Music can help us worship God in deeper ways than words alone ever could.

As you learn some of David's psalms, maybe you could sing them out loud or even in your heart to God throughout the day.

I know I am loved because...

...God gave us music and songs to praise him!

Every Good Thing

PSALM 84:1–2, 10–12

Lord of heaven's armies,
how lovely is your Temple!
I want to be in
the courtyards of the Lord's Temple.
My whole being wants
to be with the living God....
One day in the courtyards of your Temple
is better
than a thousand days anywhere else.
I would rather be a doorkeeper in the
Temple of my God
than live in the homes of the wicked.
The Lord God is like our sun and shield.
The Lord gives us kindness
and glory.

He does not hold back
anything good
from those whose life
is innocent.
Lord of heaven's armies,
happy are the people
who trust you!

Precious Promises

Look around you. What do you see? A teacher? Friends? A home? Family? Clothes? God's creation?

Everywhere we look, we see the beauty of God's love shining toward us. He even says it plainly in his Word, the Bible. God loves his kids! He wants the very best for you. That's why he promises to never hold back good things from those who love him. Of course, what God says is good may be different from what you had in mind. But his ways are always best and true. Trust his heart. Thank him today for being the giver of all good things.

I know I am loved because . . .

. . . God gives me good things!

Forever and Ever, Amen

ord, you have been our home
since the beginning.
Before the mountains were born,
and before you created the earth
and the world,
you are God.
You have always been, and you
will always be.
You turn people back into dust.
You say, "Go back into dust, human
beings."
To you, a thousand years
Is like the passing of a day.
It passes like an hour in the night....

Teach us how short our lives really are
      so that we may be wise.
Lord, how long before you return
      and show kindness to your servants?
Fill us with your love every morning.
      Then we will sing and rejoice all our
         lives.
We have seen years of trouble.
      Now give us joy as you gave us sorrow.
Show your servants the wonderful things
      you do.
      Show your greatness to our children.
Lord our God, be pleased with us.
      Give us success in what we do.
      Yes, give us success in what we do.

Perfect Princess Praise

When was the last time your parents bought you a new pair of shoes? How about a pack of gum or candy bar? A video game? Some things last longer than others. But nothing that you buy lasts forever.

That's why the Bible tells us not to put our hope in the things of this world. Instead, we should always remember God. He has always been around. He always will be here with us. He has also created people who will live forever—

either with him or without him. Praise God for being holy! Thank him, too, for sending Jesus. When we love and accept Jesus, we can live forever with him.

I know I am loved because...
...God's love for me lasts forever!

Avoiding Evil

I will sing of love and fairness.
Lord, I will sing praises to you.
I will be careful to live an innocent life.
When will you come to me?
I will live an innocent life in my house.
I will not look at anything wicked.
I hate those who turn against you.
They will not be found near me.
Let those who want to do wrong stay
away from me.
I will have nothing to do with evil.
If anyone secretly says things against
his neighbor,
I will stop him.

Faithful Love

I will not allow people
    to be proud and look down on others.
I will look for trustworthy people
    so I can live with them in the land.
Only those who live innocent lives
    will be my servants.
No one who is dishonest will live in my
       house.
    No liars will stay around me.

Faithful Love

You know your mom told you not to
eat any junk before dinner. So why are
you wandering around in the kitchen?

Sometimes it's easier to avoid bad
choices when you can walk away from
them. Get away from the thing that
might make you do something wrong.
And the advice goes beyond just food.
Do you have friends who encourage
you to do wrong? Stay away. Are there
TV shows that paint a bad picture of
God or his people? Watch something

else. David says in Psalm 101 that he delights in God so much he doesn't even want to be near bad things. We need to ask God for David's kind of faith.

I know I am loved because . . .

. . . God gives me strength to make the right choices.

Remember Me

All that I am, praise the Lord.
Everything in me, praise his
holy name.
My whole being, praise the Lord.
Do not forget all his kindnesses....
The Lord shows mercy and is kind.
He does not become angry quickly,
and he has great love.
He will not always scold us.
He will not be angry forever.
He has not punished us as our sins should
be punished.
He has not repaid us for the evil we
have done.

As high as the sky is above the earth,
so great is his love for those who
respect him.
He has taken our sins away from us
as far as the east is from the west....
The Lord's love for those who fear him
continues forever and ever.
And his goodness continues to their
grandchildren
and to those who keep his agreement
and who remember to obey his
orders.
The Lord has set his throne in heaven.
And his kingdom rules over
everything.

Precious Promises

Did you know that how you live your life is going to make a difference? The way you love God and show that to others helps people know that you are God's child. It matters today, and it will still matter long after you are grown up ...even after you are gone from this world.

God promises that his love never ends. When he chooses to love and bless you, his love is so big and powerful that it doesn't even stop there. He promises to love and care for your children and grandchildren, too. God sees the bigger picture. It's a picture of his people that includes you and all the people after you who belong to him. Imagine it's like a great big family photo! Ask God to help you live a life that leads others to him.

I know I am loved because...

...God will watch over me and my family.

Ask and Receive

appy are the people who live pure
  lives.
 They follow the Lord's teachings.
Happy are the people who keep his rules.
 They ask him for help with their
   whole heart.
They don't do what is wrong.
 They follow his ways.
Lord, you gave your orders
 to be followed completely....
How can a young person live a pure life?
 He can do it by obeying your word.
With all my heart I try to obey you, God.
 Don't let me break your commands.

150

I have taken your words to heart
    so I would not sin against you.
Lord, you should be praised.
    Teach me your demands.
My lips will tell about
    all the laws you have spoken.
I enjoy living by your rules
    as people enjoy great riches.
I think about your orders
    and study your ways.
I enjoy obeying your demands.
    And I will not forget
    your word.

Faithful Love

Faithful Love

Be honest. Do you wake up in the morning wanting to read the Bible? Does learning to remember Bible verses get you just as excited as play-time?

Don't worry. You're not alone. Faith takes time to grow. Even though learning God's Word and praying might not seem like the best use of your time—it is. As we come closer to God, our hearts begin to change. We see and understand God's beauty. He really does become our close friend. Best of

all, we can just ask God to help us love him! God knows when we are weak, and he can help make us strong!

I know I am loved because...

...God helps me remember and treasure his Word.

Heavenly Architect

f the Lord doesn't build the house,
the builders are working for
nothing.
If the Lord doesn't guard the city,
the guards are watching for nothing.
It is no use for you to get up early
and stay up late,
working for a living.
The Lord gives sleep to those
he loves.
Children are a gift from the Lord.
Babies are a reward.

Sons who are born to a young man
    are like arrows in the hand of
        a warrior.
Happy is the man
    who has his bag full of arrows.
They will not be defeated
    when they fight their enemies
        in court.

Faithful Love

Bet you didn't know God was an architect, or builder, did you? In fact, God has been building his kingdom from before time began. He has already made his plans, and he has his kids to help in the work.

Our problem is that we often forget that God is in charge. Sometimes we want to have our own way and not listen to God or our parents. We begin to believe that if we just try hard enough, we can make our dreams happen.

But God reminds us to keep our faith in the right place. Only God can help make our dreams and plans come true. Without God, we can do nothing. So trust in him and pray for his love to always be with you, just as he promises.

I know I am loved because . . .

. . . God says children are a gift from him!

Be Happy

Praise the Lord!
Sing a new song to the Lord.
Sing his praise in the meeting of his
people.
Let the Israelites be happy because of
God, their Maker.
Let the people of Jerusalem rejoice
because of their King.
They should praise him with dancing.
They should praise him with
tambourines and harps.
The Lord is pleased with his people.
He saves those who are not proud.
Let those who worship him rejoice in his
glory.
Let them sing for joy even in bed! ...

Praise the Lord!
Praise God in his Temple.
Praise him in his mighty
heaven.
Praise him for his strength.
Praise him for his greatness.
Praise him with the trumpet blasts.
Praise him with harps and lyres.
Praise him with tambourines and dancing.
Praise him with stringed instruments
and flutes.
Praise him with loud cymbals.
Praise him with crashing cymbals.
Let everything that breathes praise
the Lord.
Praise the Lord!

159

Perfect Princess Praise

When you are at a ball game and your favorite team scores, what do you do? Do you stand quietly and watch? NO! You shout, raise your hands, maybe even do a little dance.

When we are excited about something, it shows in the way we act. It shines on our faces. So why should our worship of God be any different? If we really believe that God loves and cares for us, then we should stand up and praise him! Sing out loud about God's

glory. Clap! Be happy and joyful. God delights in our praises for him!

I know I am loved so . . .

. . . I can sing and praise my God!

Walk in Wisdom

These are the wise words of Solomon son of David. Solomon was king of Israel.

They teach wisdom and self-control.

They give understanding.

They will teach you how to be wise and self-controlled.

They will teach you what is honest and fair and right.

They give the ability to think to those with little knowledge.

They give knowledge and good sense to the young.

Wise people should also listen to them and learn even more.

162

Even they will find good advice in
these words.
Then they will be able to understand wise
words and stories.
They will understand the words of
wise men and their riddles.
Knowledge begins with respect for the
Lord.
But foolish people hate wisdom and
discipline.
My child listen to your father's teaching.
And do not forget your mother's
advice.

LIVIN' THE PRINCESS LIFE

Solomon was the wisest man in the world. We can learn how to be wise from his words written in the Bible. Solomon gives us many thoughts on how to live our lives. He encourages us to understand what is really important in this life.

So what is really important, according to Solomon? Gaining wisdom. How do we gain wisdom? We can ask God for it, we can read his Word—and we can obey what we already know God has told us to do. When we obey God, we begin to think more like him. We understand why we were put here on this earth, and we are better able to make good choices that will strengthen our relationship with God. Take time right now to ask God for the desire to be wise, and start obeying him.

I know I am loved because...

...God helps me to be obedient to my parents and to him!

Divine Appointment

ISAIAH 7:14–15; LUKE 2:7–12

"The Lord himself will give you a sign: The virgin will be pregnant. She will have a son, and she will name him Immanuel. He will be eating milk curds and honey when he learns to reject what is evil and to choose what is good." …

While Joseph and Mary were in Bethlehem, the time came for her to have the baby. She gave birth to her first son. There were no rooms left in the inn. So she wrapped the baby with cloths and laid him in a box where animals are fed.

That night, some shepherds were in the fields nearby watching their sheep. An angel of the Lord stood before them. The

glory of the Lord was shining around them, and suddenly they became very frightened. The angel said to them, "Don't be afraid, because I am bringing you some good news. It will be a joy to all the people. Today your Savior was born in David's town. He is Christ, the Lord. This is how you will know him: You will find a baby wrapped in cloths and lying in a feeding box."

LIVIN' THE PRINCESS LIFE

If someone told you exactly what you would be doing 20 years from now, would you believe them? Probably not. But God knows the plan for each of his children. In fact, he planned it out even before he made the world.

Isaiah shows us a glimpse of God's plan. Although it was written many hundreds of years before Jesus was born, Isaiah tells exactly how the Savior would come to earth.

As God's princesses, we can be full of joy because we know that nothing comes into our lives by mistake. God is

close by us, working in everything that happens to us to-day. Can you see God's work in your life?

I know I am loved because . . .

. . . God has a special plan for my life!

Three's Company

Nebuchadnezzar said, "Shadrach, Meshach and Abednego, is it true that you do not serve my gods? And is it true that you did not worship the gold statue I have set up? Now, you will hear the sound of the horns, flutes, lyres, zithers, harps, pipes and all the other musical instruments. And you must be ready to bow down and worship the statue I made. That will be good. But if you do not worship it, you will be thrown quickly into the blazing furnace. Then no god will be able to save you from my power!"

Shadrach, Meshach and Abednego answered the king. They said, "Nebuchadnezzar, we do not need to defend ourselves to you. You can throw us into the blazing furnace. The God we serve is able to save us from the furnace and your power. If he does this, it is good. But even if God does not save us, we want you, our king, to know this: We will not serve your gods. We will not worship the gold statue you have set up."

Royal Connections

The Bible makes it sound so simple and easy. If they didn't obey the king, they would die. But Shadrach, Meshach, and Abednego had faith in God, and they had each other.

We should always value the importance of having friends who follow the Lord. As you go through your day playing with friends at home or at school, pay attention to what your friends are doing and saying. Do any of them talk about God? If they do, work hard to keep them as friends for a long time.

Ask God to bring others into your life who can help you make good choices and love him.

I know I am loved because . . .

. . . God sends friends who love him, too!

Living Out Loud

DANIEL 6:6-7, 9-10

The supervisors and the governors went as a group to the king. They said: "King Darius, live forever!... We think the king should make this law that everyone would have to obey: No one should pray to any god or man except to you our king. This should be done for the next 30 days. Anyone who doesn't obey will be thrown into the lions' den...." So King Darius made the law and had it written.

When Daniel heard that the new law had been written, he went to his house.

He went to his upstairs room. The windows of that room opened toward Jerusalem. Three times each day Daniel got down on his knees and prayed. He prayed and thanked God, just as he always had done.

LIVIN' THE PRINCESS LIFE

Even though Daniel knew that he could be killed by lions, he still continued to pray to God. The king ordered that no one pray to anyone other than him. Not only did Daniel keep praying to God, he prayed three times each day at the front window of his home so everyone could see! Daniel wanted the world to know that he served the only true God. He would not stop serving God just to please an earthly king.

Sometimes you might want to hide from Jesus? Do you feel like your friends might laugh if they find out you go to church or pray? Are you afraid to speak about your faith because of what people might say? Remember Daniel. He was bold about his actions because he knew they were right. You, too, can be bold in your faith, knowing that it is better to make God happy. Don't be afraid of what others think. God can help you. He can change the hearts of the same people who might not understand his ways.

I know I am loved when . . .

. . . God helps me share his ways with those around me.

Hide and Seek

The Lord spoke his word to Jonah son of Amittai: "Get up, go to the great city of Nineveh and preach against it. I see the evil things they do."

But Jonah got up to run away from the Lord. He went to the city of Joppa. There he found a ship that was going to the city of Tarshish. Jonah paid for the trip and went aboard. He wanted to go to Tarshish to run away from the Lord.

But the Lord sent a great wind on the sea. This wind made the sea very rough. So the ship was in danger of breaking apart. The sailors were afraid. Each man cried to his own god. The men began throwing the cargo into the sea. This would make the ship lighter so it would not sink.

But Jonah had gone down into the ship to lie down. He fell fast asleep. The captain of the ship came and said, "Why are you sleeping? Get up! Pray to your god! Maybe your god will pay attention to us. Maybe he will save us!"

LIVIN' THE PRINCESS LIFE

Jonah had spent a lot of energy. He was running away from God and what he had asked Jonah to do. On land, onto a boat, into a big fish, and back on land again—all of Jonah's efforts were no match for God.

We can't escape God. He is everywhere. We can't hide among our friends, our clothes, our toys, or our busy daily routines. God is still with us everywhere we go. Just like he did with Jonah, God chases after us. Instead of avoiding God, we need to turn to him in our hearts and minds as we

go about our day. When we live for
God, we discover true joy. So
don't hide from God. Enjoy
what is really life's biggest
blessing—
knowing and
following God.

I know I am loved because...
...God is with me everywhere I go!

Powerful Promise

MALACHI 3:1–4, 16–17

The Lord of heaven's armies says, "I will send my messenger. He will prepare the way for me to come. Suddenly, the Lord you are looking for will come to his Temple. The messenger of the agreement, whom you want, will come." ... He will be like a purifying fire. He will be like laundry soap. He will be like someone who heats and purifies silver. He will purify the Levites. He will make them pure like gold and silver. Then they will bring offerings to the Lord in the right way. And he will accept the offerings from Judah and Jerusalem. It will be as it was in the past. ...

Then those who honored the Lord spoke with each other. The Lord listened and heard them. The names of those who honored the Lord and respected him were written in a book. The Lord will remember them.

The Lord of heaven's armies says, "They belong to me. On that day they will be my very own. A father shows mercy to his son who serves him. In the same way I will show mercy to my people."

LIVIN' THE PRINCESS LIFE

From the time of Adam's sin in the garden, people have been waiting. They were waiting for God's promise of a Savior who would free us from sin. Finally, after thousands of years had passed, Jesus did come to earth. He paid for our sins on the cross. But when he rose again and went to heaven, Jesus mentioned another promise that Malachi told about hundreds of years before. He promised to come again one day to gather his people together.

Like the Hebrews of long ago, we are waiting. Even though it may take a long time, we still wait with hope. God has promised Jesus will come again. We don't know when that day will be. But let's live our lives like he will be here today!

I know I am loved because . . .

. . . Jesus promised to return again!

The Sword of Truth

The Spirit led Jesus into the desert to be tempted by the devil. Jesus ate nothing for 40 days and nights. After this, he was very hungry. The devil came to Jesus to tempt him. The devil said, "If you are the Son of God, tell these rocks to become bread."

Jesus answered, "It is written in the Scriptures, 'A person does not live only by eating bread. But a person lives by everything the Lord says.'"

Then the devil led Jesus to the holy city of Jerusalem. He put Jesus on a very high place of the Temple. The devil said, "If you are the Son of God, jump off...."

Jesus answered him, "It also says in the Scriptures, 'Do not test the Lord your God.'" The devil led Jesus to the top of a very high mountain. He showed Jesus all the kingdoms of the world and all the great things that are in those kingdoms. The devil said, "If you will bow down and worship me, I will give you all these things."

Jesus said to the devil, "Go away from me, Satan! It is written in the Scriptures, 'You must worship the Lord your God. Serve only him!'"

187

Satan had the perfect plan. First, he would try to get Jesus to sin when he was weak from hunger. Then he tried to get Jesus to prove he was God's Son. Again, Jesus stood firm. Finally, Satan offered Jesus the world, if Jesus would just bow to him. But Jesus won the battle every time.

Notice anything special about Jesus' words to Satan? What do they have in common? Yes, they all came from the Bible. Jesus fought Satan using the truth of God's Word. That's exactly how we should fight him, too. We can't outsmart Satan and his crafty temptations alone. God gives us wisdom through his Word. Wisdom helps us defeat the devil if he ever tempts us to make wrong choices. That's why we should work hard to keep what God has said in our hearts.

I know I am loved because...

...God gave me his Word to help me be strong!

Loving God

MATTHEW 25:34–40

The King will say to the good people on his right, "Come, My Father has given you his blessing. Come and receive the kingdom God has prepared for you since the world was made. I was hungry, and you gave me food. I was thirsty, and you gave me something to drink. I was alone and away from home, and you invited me into your house. I was without clothes, and you gave me something to wear. I was sick, and you cared for me. I was in prison, and you visited me."

Then the good people will answer, "Lord, when did we see you hungry and give you food? When did we see you

thirsty and give you something to drink?
When did we see you alone and away
from home and invite you into our house?
When did we see you without clothes and
give you something to wear? When did we
see you sick or in prison and care for you?"

Then the King will answer, "I tell you
the truth. Anything you did for any of my
people here, you also did for me."

Royal Connections

How can you love a spirit? We can't see God or touch him. We certainly can't put our arms around him to give him a big hug. So how do we really love God?

We love God with our lives. The way we care for others. The way we help feed the poor, or make friends with those who are lonely. When we care for the sick, or when we obey our parents, we show God how we love him. When we spend time thinking about God and his Word, and when we sing praises to him or pray, God knows we love him.

Everything we do in life can be a way
to love him, if we make
him the reason why
we do what we do.

I know I am loved because...

...God provides for me and my family!

Our Lifeline

esus and his followers went to a place called Gethsemane. He said to his followers, "Sit here while I pray." Jesus told Peter, James, and John to come with him. Then Jesus began to be very sad and troubled. He said to them, "I am full of sorrow. My heart is breaking with sadness. Stay here and watch."

Jesus walked a little farther away from them. Then he fell on the ground and prayed. He prayed that, if possible, he would not have this time of suffering. He prayed, "Abba, Father! You can do all things. Let me not have this cup of suffering. But do what you want, not what I want."

Then Jesus went back to his followers. He found them asleep. He said to Peter, "Simon, why are you sleeping? You could not stay awake with me for one hour? Stay awake and pray that you will not be tempted. Your spirit wants to do what is right, but your body is weak."

Again Jesus went away and prayed the same thing. Then he went back to the followers. Again he found them asleep because their eyes were very heavy. And they did not know what to say to Jesus.

LIVIN' THE PRINCESS LIFE

Have you ever wondered why Jesus prayed? Jesus did only the things that his Father told him to do. We see Jesus many times waking up early or escaping the crowds to pray. That shows how important it was to Jesus to stay connected to the Father.

Prayer is not just a nice idea, or what we do when we want something. It is our lifeline to stay connected with our heavenly Father, just like Jesus did. God gives us the gift of prayer to help us and other people around us. Prayer keeps us trusting in God and relying on him. It is the way we can ask God for help, too. The Bible says we should always be ready to pray to God.

I know I am loved because...

...God gave me the lifeline of prayer to him!

Best Friends for Life

"Remember the teaching of Moses my servant. I gave those laws and rules to him at Mount Sinai. They are for all Israelites.

"But I will send Elijah the prophet to you. He will come before that great and terrible day of the Lord's judging. Elijah will help fathers love their children. And he will help the children love their fathers."...

"John will be a great man for the Lord. He will never drink wine or beer. Even at the time John is born, he will be filled with the Holy Spirit. He will help many

people of Israel return to the Lord their
God. He himself will go first before the
Lord. John will be powerful in spirit like
Elijah. He will make
peace between
fathers and
their children.
He will bring
those who are not
obeying God back
to the right way of
thinking. He will make
people ready for the coming of the Lord."

They were there when you were born.
They stayed up with you through
countless nights. They fed you,
changed your diapers, played silly
games with you, and watched you
grow. Your parents know more about
you than you do. If they're like most
parents, they love you more than you'll
ever know. Your parents are a precious
gift from God.

So don't take his gift and misuse it.
Don't be mean or disrespectful toward

your parents. If you let them, they can become your very best friends who will encourage you and love you through the rest of your life.

I know I am loved because . . .

. . . God shows his love for me through my parents!

Each One Matters

Jesus told them this story: "Suppose one of you has 100 sheep but he loses 1 of them. Then he will leave the other 99 sheep alone and go out and look for the lost sheep. The man will keep on searching for the lost sheep until he finds it. And when he finds it, the man is very happy.... In the same way, I tell you there is much joy in heaven when 1 sinner changes his heart. There is more joy for that 1 sinner than there is for 99 good people who don't need to change.

"Suppose a woman has ten silver coins, but she loses one of them. She will light a

lamp and clean the house. She will look carefully for the coin until she finds it. And when she finds it, she will call her friends and neighbors and say, 'Be happy with me because I have found the coin that was lost!' In the same way, there is joy before the angels of God when 1 sinner changes his heart."

LIVIN' THE PRINCESS LIFE

Come on! You have 99 other sheep. Do you really need to go looking for the 1 that always wanders off? Or 10 coins—will you really miss just 1? According to Jesus and the way he sees his people, the answer is yes!

Jesus said that all of heaven rejoices when just 1 of his children who has made bad choices changes their ways and turns to God. But do you know what's really amazing about the stories of the lost sheep and the lost coin? Neither the lost sheep nor the lost coin was worried about finding their master. They were simply lost without hope of being found — until the owner got busy looking for them. Isn't it amazing that God chases after us to show us his love? He finds us, and he changes our hearts. His family is just not complete without all his children. Thank God today for finding you and drawing you into his family.

I know I am loved because ...
... God has made me a part of his loving family!

Mystery Solved

"The only one who has ever gone up to heaven is the One who came down from heaven—the Son of Man.

"Moses lifted up the snake in the desert. It is the same with the Son of Man. The Son of Man must be lifted up too. Then everyone who believes in him can have eternal life.

"For God loved the world so much that he gave his only Son. God gave his Son so that whoever believes in him may not be lost, but have eternal life. God did not send his Son into the world to judge the world guilty, but to save the world through him. He who believes in God's Son is not judged guilty. He who does not

believe has already been judged guilty, because he has not believed in God's only Son. People are judged by this fact: I am the Light from God that has come into the world. But men did not want the light. They wanted darkness because they were doing evil things. Everyone who does evil hates the light. He will not come to the light because it will show all the evil things he has done. But he who follows the true way comes to the light. Then the light will show that the things he has done were done through God."

How do you know you're going to heaven? Do you try to be good enough for God to like you? Don't worry. Let John 3:16 remove your doubt.

God makes it really clear that salvation—being saved from your sins and getting to go to heaven—is a free gift. When we receive his gift, we don't have to worry anymore. Anyone who is trusting in Jesus alone to get to heaven will go there. How do you know he's in your heart? You ask him to come in to forgive you and change you. And he will! He promises to do it. Just keep looking to him to help you believe in him. Let him make you into the person he wants you to be.

I know I am loved because...

...God gave me the gift of his Son, Jesus!

Baalieve It

"The one who enters by the door is the shepherd of the sheep. The man who guards the door opens it for him. And the sheep listen to the voice of the shepherd. He calls his own sheep, using their names, and he leads them out. He brings all of his sheep out. Then he goes ahead of them and leads them. They follow him because they know his voice."...

"I am the good shepherd. The good shepherd gives his life for the sheep. The worker who is paid to keep the sheep is different from the shepherd who owns them.... He does not really care for the sheep.

"I am the good shepherd. I know my sheep, and my sheep know me, just as the Father knows me, and I know the Father. I give my life for the sheep. I have other sheep that are not in this flock here. I must bring them also. They will listen to my voice, and there will be one flock and one shepherd. The Father loves me because I give my life. I give my life so that I can take it back again. No one takes it away from me. I give my own life freely. I have the right to take it back. This is what my Father commanded me to do."...

Children, obey your parents in all things. This pleases the Lord.

Want to know something funny about sheep? They're not too smart. They don't know where they're going. They make the same mistakes again and again. And if they fall over, someone must pick them up. Want to know something else? God says that we are

his sheep! He knows that we need help, guidance, and direction. So he gives it to us through his Word—and through our parents. God says that children must obey their parents, just like sheep must follow the shepherd. Obeying our parents not only honors God, it also keeps us safe.

I know I am loved because...

...God guides and directs me!

The Perfect Gift

ACTS 3:2-3, 6-8

At the Temple gate called Beautiful Gate, was a man who had been crippled all his life. Every day he was carried to this gate to beg. He would ask for money from the people going into the Temple. The man saw Peter and John going into the Temple and asked them for money.... But Peter said, "I don't have any silver or gold, but I do have something else I can give you: By the power of Jesus Christ from Nazareth—stand up and walk!" Then Peter took the man's right hand and lifted him up. Immediately the man's feet

and ankles became strong. He jumped up, stood on his feet, and began to walk. He went into the Temple with them, walking and jumping, and praising God.

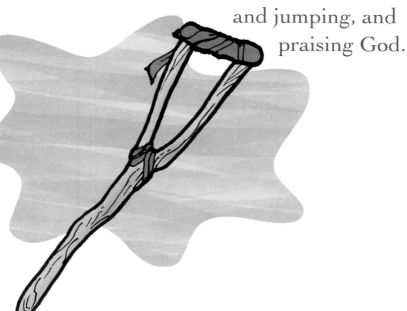

LIVIN' THE PRINCESS LIFE

Some people can sing. Others dance. Some are really smart, while others are funny. And some people don't seem to feel special at all. Maybe you feel that way sometimes. Peter and John, two of Jesus' disciples, may have felt that way, too.

One day they passed by a crippled man who begged them for help. They admitted that they didn't have money or anything natural to offer the man. But what they could give him was heal-ing power from God. When God made his crippled legs well again, his whole soul was healed.

No matter what sort of special things you have or may not have, God can use you to do mighty things for his kingdom. Remember that there is nothing better you can give to the world than the message of hope and love found in Christ Jesus.

I know I am loved because...

...I am special through God's hope and love.

Team Boosters

EXODUS 20:12; ACTS 15:30–33, 35

"onor your father and your mother. Then you will live a long time in the land."...

The men left Jerusalem and went to Antioch. There they gathered the church and gave them the letter. When they read it, they were very happy because of the encouraging letter. Judas and Silas were also prophets, who said many things to encourage the believers and make them stronger. After some time Judas and Silas were sent off in peace by the believers. They went back to those who had sent them....

But Paul and Barnabas stayed in Antioch. They and many others preached the Good News and taught the people the message of the Lord.

What's the first thing you do after you've painted a picture? You show it to your parents, hoping they'll tell you how great it is. Or when you play a sport, you count on them to cheer for you from the sidelines.

But have you ever thought about who cheers for your parents? They are people, just like you. They also want to be encouraged. They need to know that they are doing a good job. Just one word from you, telling them you appreciate their hard work will brighten their whole day. We bless God, our parents, and everyone around us when we say nice things to make them happy.

I know I am loved because...
...God gives me the heart to help make people happy!

The Cure

I am not ashamed of the Good News. It is the power God uses to save everyone who believes—to save the Jews first, and then to save the non-Jews. The Good News shows how God makes people right with himself. God's way of making people right with him begins and ends with faith. As the Scripture says, "The person who is made right with God by faith will live forever."...

God makes people right with himself through their faith in Jesus Christ. This is true for all who believe in Christ, because all are the same. All people have sinned

and are not good enough for God's glory.
People are made right with God by his
grace, which is a free gift. They are made
right with God by being made free from
sin through Jesus Christ. God sent him to
die in our place to take away our sins. We
receive forgiveness through faith. And all
of this is because of the blood of Jesus'
death....

Good News

Royal Connections

If your friend had a terrible disease and could possibly die, and you had the medicine that would cure him, would you give it to him? Of course!

Right now, all around us, the world is dying. People don't know or believe in Jesus. They are headed for eternal life apart from God. But we have the cure. We can tell them that God has made a way for us to live forever, just like it says in the Bible — by trusting in his Son. We don't need to be scared or embarrassed by telling them the truth.

We know if they listen and believe their very lives will be saved. Who do you need to share this Good News with today? Pray for them, and tell them about God's love.

I know I am loved because...

...God gives me strength to share his Good News with others.

Fit for Royalty

Do not owe people anything. But you will always owe love to each other. The person who loves others has obeyed all the law. The law says, "You must not be guilty of adultery. You must not murder anyone. You must not steal. You must not want to take your neighbor's things." All these commands and all others are really only one rule: "Love your neighbor as you love yourself." Love never hurts a neighbor. So loving is obeying all the law.

I say this because we live in an important time. Yes, it is now time for you to wake up from your sleep. Our salvation is nearer now than when we first believed.

The "night" is almost finished. The "day" is almost here. So we should stop doing things that belong to darkness and take up the weapons used for fighting in the light. Let us live in a right way, like people who belong to the day.... Clothe yourselves with the Lord Jesus Christ. Forget about satisfying your sinful self.

LIVIN' THE PRINCESS LIFE

So what does it look like to be a Christian? Is it special clothes or outfits? No, it looks like someone who has given his or her life to the Lord Jesus. How can we give our lives when we're still living and growing? God says that we should obey him in everything we do, say, and even think. That means asking him for help to live a holy life. Ask him to help you stay away from making wrong choices and be strong to make the right ones.

When you understand what an incredible gift it is to be God's friend — his own princess — you will want to do what pleases him. It will bring you joy to bring God joy. So start acting like the child of the King you really are!

I know I am loved because...

...I am a child of the King!!

Join the Team!

We are only servants of God who helped you believe. Each one of us did the work God gave us to do. I planted the seed of the teaching in you, and Apollos watered it. But God is the One who made the seed grow. So the one who plants is not important, and the one who waters is not important. Only God is important, because he is the One who makes things grow. The one who plants and the one who waters have the same purpose. And each will be rewarded for his own work. We are workers together for God. And you are like a farm that belongs to God.

And you are a house that belongs to God. Like an expert builder I built the foundation of that house. I used the gift that God gave me to do this. Others are building on that foundation. But everyone should be careful how he builds. The foundation has already been built. No one can build any other foundation. The foundation that has already been laid is Jesus Christ.

LIVIN' THE PRINCESS LIFE

Helping other people know Jesus
might seem to be an impossible task.
And if you're trying to do it on your
own, it will be!

The great news about God's kingdom
is that it's a team effort. God uses each
of us in different ways right where we
are to help tell others about Jesus. You
don't have to tell everything you know
about God to someone you just met.
Pray for God's help to always be ready
to say just the right thing when the time

comes. He promises to give you wisdom right when you need it. Then God will have another Christian share a little bit more with that person. In God's perfect timing, he will change that person's heart and they will see his love.

I know I am loved when...
...I'm happy to share God with others.

Joyful Givers

2 CORINTHIANS 9:6-12

emember this: The person who plants a little will have a small harvest. But the person who plants a lot will have a big harvest. Each one should give, then, what he has decided in his heart to give. He should not give if it makes him sad. And he should not give if he thinks he is forced to give. God loves the person who gives happily. And God can give you more blessings than you need. Then you will always have plenty of everything. You will have enough to give to every good work. It is written in the Scriptures:

"He gives freely to the poor.
The things he does are right and
will continue forever."

God is the One who gives seed to the
farmer. And he gives bread for food. And
God will give you all the seed you need
and make it grow. He will make a great
harvest from your goodness. God will
make you rich in every way so that you
can always give freely. And your giving
through us will cause many to give thanks
to God. This service that you do helps the
needs of God's people. It is also bringing
more and more thanks to God.

LIVIN' THE PRINCESS LIFE

Picture this: You have been saving up for weeks to buy something you really want. You've earned just about what you need. Then you go to Sunday school and a missionary tells your class about the poor children where he serves. They need money just to have enough to eat or clothes to wear. What will you do?

Jesus says that we should give some of the money we earn back to him. This is called a tithe. But he also encourages us to give more than what we simply "owe" God. He wants us to have hearts that love to give, and give happily. When we put God first and want to help we will be happy to give to others who need us. Giving to those in need keeps us from making material things too important in our lives. It allows us to bless others.

I know I am loved because . . .

. . . God helps me to be a cheerful, happy giver!

A+ for Effort

Anyone who is learning the teaching of God should share all the good things he has with his teacher.

Do not be fooled: You cannot cheat God. A person harvests only what he plants.... If he plants to please the Spirit, he will receive eternal life from the Spirit. We must not become tired of doing good. We will receive our harvest of eternal life at the right time. We must not give up! When we have the opportunity to help anyone, we should do it. But we should give special attention to those who are in the family of believers.

LIVIN' THE PRINCESS LIFE

Have you ever thought about what it would be like to be a teacher? There you are, standing in front of a class of kids—some who care what you have to say and others who don't. Because we have so many teachers helping us, it's easy to not take the time to appreciate them or thank them.

But teachers are special to God, especially the teachers who help others come to know him better. In fact, Galatians 6:6 tells us that we should share every good thing we have with our teachers! That means if we have a special gift, we should share it with them. If we learned something new and exciting, we should let our teachers know. Most importantly, we must do what they say. It will make their hearts happy to know that their teaching is worth all the hard work they do!

I know I am loved because...
...God gives me good teachers to help me learn.

Prayer's Power Source

bow in prayer before the Father. Every family in heaven and on earth gets its true name from him. I ask the Father in his great glory to give you the power to be strong in spirit. He will give you that strength through his Spirit. I pray that Christ will live in your hearts because of your faith. I pray that your life will be strong in love and be built on love. And I pray that you and all God's holy people will have the power to understand the greatness of Christ's love. I pray that you can understand how wide and how long and how high and how deep that love is.

Christ's love is greater than any person can ever know. But I pray that you will be able to know that love. Then you can be filled with the fullness of God.

With God's power working in us, God can do much, much more than anything we can ask or think of.

Suddenly, something comes up and you need help. The problem is so big you're not even sure how to pray about it. What can you do? Well, you could worry — but that won't help things. God tells us not to worry, but to instead take everything to him in prayer. You know why?

God is a big God. He is bigger than your problems, and even bigger than your imagination. It's hard to even begin to understand how powerful he really is. So when he says he can help

you, believe him! Take whatever is on your heart to him in prayer. Then leave it with him. Stop worrying. Wait for God to act. Trust that his answer will be the very best for you—whether it's the answer you want or not.

I know I am loved because...

...God can take care of my worries!

Lovin' Out Loud

EPHESIANS 5:1-2, 6-17, 19-20

You are God's children whom he loves. So try to be like God. Live a life of love. Love other people just as Christ loved us. Christ gave himself for us—he was a sweet-smelling offering and sacrifice to God....

Do not let anyone fool you by telling you things that are not true. These things will bring God's anger on those who do not obey him. So have no part with them. In the past you were full of darkness, but now you are full of light in the Lord. So live like children who belong to the light. Light brings every kind of goodness, right living, and truth. Try to learn what pleases the Lord. Do not do the things that people in darkness do. That brings nothing good. But do good things to show that the things done in darkness are wrong. It is shameful even to talk about what those people do in secret. But the light makes all things easy to see. And everything that is made easy to see can become light....

So be very careful how you live. Do not live like those who are not wise. Live wisely. I mean that you should use every chance you have for doing good, because these are evil times. So do not be foolish with your lives. But learn what the Lord wants you to do.... Speak to each other with psalms, hymns, and spiritual songs. Sing and make music in your hearts to the Lord. Always give thanks to God the Father for everything, in the name of our Lord Jesus Christ.

Satan really hates to hear us sing. Why?
Because God loves to hear our praises.
It's almost as if we can feel him right
there with us when we sing. God heals
our hearts and brings us closer to him
when we praise him.

So what kind of day have you had?
Whether you're feeling down in the

dumps or excited about life, turn your eyes to Jesus, who gives all good things. Listen to your favorite CD or Christian radio station. Or just sing out loud all on your own. Praising God is a great way to lift our spirits and our love to the one who matters most.

I know I am loved especially . . .
. . . when I praise my Father God!

What a Joy!

God is working in you to help you want to do what pleases him. Then he gives you the power to do it.

Do everything without complaining or arguing. Then you will be innocent and without anything wrong in you. You will be God's children without fault. But you are living with crooked and mean people all around you. Among them you shine like stars in the dark world. You offer to them the teaching that gives life. So when Christ comes again, I can be happy because my work was not wasted. I ran in the race and won.

250

Your faith makes you offer your lives as a sacrifice in serving God. Perhaps I will have to offer my own blood with your sacrifice. But if that happens, I will be happy and full of joy with all of you. You also should be happy and full of joy with me. . . .

Be full of joy in the Lord. It is not trouble for me to write the same things to you again, and it will help you to be more ready.

LIVIN' THE PRINCESS LIFE

How can you spot a Christian who really has a close friendship with God? You'll see it on their face. You'll hear it in their voice. They have joy in their heart because they love the Lord. It's the one quality that amazes everyone else. But when Paul said that we should always be joyful, he didn't mean that we should be happy all the time. There are times of sadness in everyone's life.

Joy goes deeper. Even in hard times we know that, in the end, things will get better. One day we will be with Jesus.

Even now, in this difficult time, Jesus is right by our side. Knowing that Jesus is still in control and loves us—even when everything seems to be going wrong—brings us a joy that never goes away.

I know I am loved when...

...having God in my heart brings me joy!

e full of joy in the Lord always. I will say again, be full of joy.

Let all men see that you are gentle and kind. The Lord is coming soon. Do not worry about anything. But pray and ask God for everything you need. And when you pray, always give thanks. And God's peace will keep your hearts and minds in Christ Jesus. The peace that God gives is so great that we cannot understand it. . . .

I have learned to be satisfied with the things I have and with everything that happens. I know how to live when I am poor. And I know how to live when I have plenty. I have learned the secret of being happy at any time in everything that happens. I have learned to be happy when I have enough to eat and when I do not have enough to eat. I have learned to be happy when I have all that I need and when I do not have the things I need. I can do all things through Christ because he gives me strength.

Royal Connections

There's no doubt it's hard. At times, it seems impossible to love your brother or sister. After all, don't all siblings fight? Isn't that just the way it is?

It's not the way God wants it to be. He wants us to have peaceful homes. He wants us to show the same kind of love Jesus shows us. So how can you love your little sister when she calls you a name? Or when your older brother locks you in your room? Pray! Ask God for help. Ask him to give you his love,

and to help you remember the good things about your siblings. Then answer them the way God wants you to—no matter what they say back.

I know I am loved when...

...God helps me get along with my family.

Making Wrongs Right

COLOSSIANS 3:8–10, 12–17

Put these things out of your life: anger, bad temper, doing or saying things to hurt others, and using evil words when you talk. Do not lie to each other. You have left your old sinful life and the things you did before. You have begun to live the new life. In your new life you are being made new. You are becoming like the One who made you. This new life brings you the true knowledge of God....

God has chosen you and made you his holy people. He loves you. So always do these things: Show mercy to others; be kind, humble, gentle, and patient. Do not be angry with each other, but forgive each other. If someone does wrong to you, then forgive him. Forgive each other because the Lord forgave you. Do all these things; but most important, love each other. Love is what holds you all together in perfect unity. Let the peace that Christ gives control your thinking. You were all called together in one body to have peace. Always be thankful. Let the teaching of Christ live in you richly. Use all wisdom to teach and strengthen each other. Sing psalms, hymns, and spiritual songs with thankfulness in your hearts to God. Everything you say and everything you do should all be done for Jesus your Lord. And in all you do, give thanks to God the Father through Jesus.

You knew it was wrong, but you did it anyway. Now the Holy Spirit helps you realize you have to admit your wrong choice. You've got to make things right again with God and your parents, but you're scared. What should you do?

Pray. Confess it to God and ask for forgiveness. Then ask God for the right time to tell your parents. Remember, punishments only last a short time. Your parents will be glad you were honest and told the truth. They will help you recover from your mistake, and love you for admitting it.

I know I am loved because . . .

. . . God forgives me of my wrong choices when I ask him.

Walk the Talk

Do all you can to live a peaceful life. Take care of your own business. Do your own work. We have already told you to do these things. If you do, then people who are not believers will respect you. And you will not have to depend on others for what you need....

Now brothers, we ask you to respect those people who work hard with you, who lead you in the Lord and teach you. Respect them with a very special love because of the work they do with you.

Live in peace with each other. We ask you, brothers, to warn those who do not

work. Encourage the people who are afraid. Help those who are weak. Be patient with every person. Be sure that no one pays back wrong for wrong. But always try to do what is good for each other and for all people.

LIVIN' THE PRINCESS LIFE

Did you know that we can tell another person the Good News about Jesus without even saying a word?

God's Word says that we can show God's love to other people who don't know him by the way we act. We need to remember that the way we talk, love, forgive, and spend our time says a lot more about what's really in our hearts than just what we say. People who don't know God will see that our lives are different and better because we obey what God says in his Word. Then they can ask us why we are the way we are. We can tell them everything that Jesus has done to save us. It's much easier for them to believe us when our words match the way we behave.

I know I am loved . . .

. . . and can show that to others by the way I act and talk about God!

Parent Support

1 THESSALONIANS 5:16–25

lways be happy. Never stop praying. Give thanks whatever happens. That is what God wants for you in Christ Jesus.

Do not stop the work of the Holy Spirit. Do not treat prophecy as if it were not important. But test everything. Keep what is good. And stay away from everything that is evil.

We pray that God himself, the God of peace, will make you pure, belonging only to him. We pray that your whole self—spirit, soul, and body—will be kept safe and be without wrong when our Lord

Jesus Christ comes. The One who calls you will do that for you. You can trust him. Brothers, please pray for us.

Paul was a smart man. He knew God's Word. He had started churches and shared Jesus with lots of people. Yet there was one thing he truly needed—one thing he asked the believers for over and over. What was it? Prayer! Paul needed their prayers because he knew that his success depended completely on God, not his own efforts.

When you look at your parents, you might not think they really need you — but they do. They need you to pray for them. Pray that they will raise you in God's wisdom. Pray that they will honor God in all their decisions. Make it a daily habit to pray for your parents. Start right now.

I know I am loved because...

...God gave me parents and a family to pray for!

Remember

You are saved by the Spirit that makes you holy and by your faith in the truth. God used the Good News that we preached to call you to be saved. He called you so that you can share in the glory of our Lord Jesus Christ. So, brothers, stand strong and continue to believe the teachings we gave you. We taught you those things in our speaking and in our letter to you.

We pray that the Lord Jesus Christ himself and God our Father will comfort you and strengthen you in every good thing you do and say. God loved us. Through his grace he gave us a good hope and comfort that continues forever.

And now, brothers, pray for us. Pray that the Lord's teaching will continue to spread quickly. And pray that people will give honor to that teaching, just as happened with you. And pray that we will be protected from bad and evil people. (Not all people believe in the Lord.)

But the Lord is faithful. He will give you strength and protect you from the Evil One. The Lord makes us feel sure that you are doing the things we told you. And we know that you will continue to do those things. We pray that the Lord will lead your hearts into God's love and Christ's patience.

Every now and then some of them may come to your church and tell you interesting stories about faraway places. Sometimes you might even see their pictures on a bulletin board. But more often we forget about the missionaries who are working to help other people know about Jesus.

God tells us in his Word that we need to remember our missionaries. We should help them do their jobs by praying for them. We need to pray for their protection, and that they will have the right words to share Jesus with others.

Ask your parents to help you pick a special missionary for each week or month of the year, and pray for their needs to be met by God.

I know I am loved when...

...I share my prayers for God's special missionaries to show I love them!

Kid Power

You will show that you are made strong by the words of faith and good teaching that you have been following. People tell silly stories that do not agree with God's truth. Do not follow what those stories teach. But teach yourself only to serve God. Training your body helps you in some ways, but serving God helps you in every way. Serving God brings you blessings in this life and in the future life, too. What I say is true, and you should fully accept it. For this is why we work and struggle: We hope in the living God. He is the Savior of all people. And in a very special way, he is the Savior of all who believe in him.

Command and teach these things. You are young, but do not let anyone treat you as if you were not important. Be an example to show the believers how they should live. Show them with your words, with the way you live, with your love, with your faith, and with your pure life. Continue to read the Scriptures to the people, strengthen them, and teach them. Do these things until I come.

God's Helper

LIVIN' THE PRINCESS LIFE

Do you ever get tired of hearing grown-ups tell you you're too young to do certain things? Sometimes it can make you feel unimportant—or that life will get really fun only when you're older.

But that's not the way the apostle Paul saw it. He had a helper named Timothy who was very young to be in the ministry. It may have been easy for adults to think he was just another kid and they really shouldn't listen to him. But Paul told Timothy not to let them ignore what he was saying just because of his age. He told him that, by living the right way and speaking the truth, he could be a part of God's most important work. Even as a young princess you can, too!

I know I am loved ...

... and special even though I am young!

Protect Your Treasure

1 TIMOTHY 6:11–14, 18–21

Try to live in the right way, serve God, have faith, love, patience, and gentleness. Keeping your faith is like running a race. Try as hard as you can to win. Be sure you receive the life that continues forever. You were called to have that life. And you confessed the great truth about Christ in a way that many people heard. Before God and Christ Jesus I give you a command.... Now I tell you: Do the things you were commanded to do. Do them without wrong or blame until the time when our Lord Jesus Christ comes again....

Tell the rich people to do good and to be rich in doing good deeds. Tell them to be

LIVIN' THE PRINCESS LIFE

happy to give and ready to share. By doing that, they will be saving a treasure for themselves in heaven. That treasure will be a strong foundation. Their future life can be built on that treasure. Then they will be able to have the life that is true life.

Timothy, God has trusted you with many things. Keep those things safe. Stay away from people who say foolish things that are not from God. Stay away from those who argue against the truth. They use something they call "knowledge," but it is really not knowledge. They say that they have that "knowledge," but they have left the true faith.

LIVIN' THE PRINCESS LIFE

If someone gave you a million dollars, you wouldn't just stick it in your pocket. You'd find a safe place to put it where it wouldn't get lost or stolen.

God's truth is worth a whole lot more than any amount of money. We need to protect the truth that we've been taught. We can't store it in a bank, but we can hide it in our hearts.

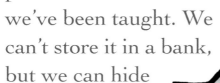

Then we must stay on our guard. We have to watch out for anyone who might want to take the truth from us by teaching us lies instead. Others may sound smart with their ideas, but if what they think goes against God, we must stay away from them. We must hold tightly to the truth of God's Word.

I know I am loved because...

...God tells me so in his Word!

Watch Out!

ou were all called by God. God sent Jesus to us, and he is the high priest of our faith. And Jesus was faithful to God as Moses was. Moses did everything God wanted him to do in God's family. A man who is the head of a family receives more honor than others in the family. It is the same with Jesus. Jesus should have more honor than Moses. Every family has its head, but God is the head of everything. Moses was faithful in God's family as a servant. He told what God would say in the future. But Christ is faithful as a Son who is the head of God's family. And

we are God's family if we hold on to our faith and are proud of the great hope we have. . . .

Be careful that none of you has an evil, unbelieving heart. This will stop you from following the living God. But encourage each other every day. Do this while it is "today." Help each other so that none of you will become hardened because of sin and its tricks. We all share in Christ. This is true if we keep till the end the sure faith we had in the beginning.

LIVIN' THE PRINCESS LIFE

When we're young, most of us have teachable hearts. Our parents and teachers can teach us right from wrong. They explain what God has said in his Word. As we grow older, we experience more of life, including good and hard times. When the hard times come, we may begin to question whether or not what we were taught as very little children really is true.

God says to watch out! It's okay to ask questions about the Bible to find out what God says. But we must ask God to help us keep hearts that believe in him.

Without faith it is impossible to please God. If we get confused, we need to turn to God right away for help. We can ask someone we trust who knows the Bible to help explain things better. Then we must listen to the truth and believe it.

I know I am loved ...

... and can trust the truth of God's teachings!

Anchor's Away

God made a promise to Abraham. And as there is no one greater than God, he used himself when he swore to Abraham. He said, "I will surely bless you and give you many descendants." Abraham waited patiently for this to happen. And he received what God promised.

People always use the name of someone greater than themselves when they swear. The oath proves that what they say is true. And this ends all arguing about what they say. God wanted to prove that his promise was true. He wanted to prove this to those who would get what he promised. He wanted them to understand clearly that his purposes never change. So God proved his promise by also making an oath. These two things cannot change. God cannot lie when he makes a promise, and he cannot lie when he makes an oath. These things encourage us who came to God for safety. They give us strength to hold on to the hope we have been given. We have this hope as an anchor for the soul, sure and strong. It enters behind the curtain in the

Most Holy Place in heaven. Jesus has gone in there ahead of us and for us. He has become the high priest forever. . . .

LIVIN' THE PRINCESS LIFE

Have you ever seen a boat or been on one? When it's time to stop moving, the captain lets down the anchor to keep the boat from getting off course.

We have an anchor, too, as God's children. It's not made out of metal, but out of the truth we find in God's Word. His promise to forgive us and never leave us becomes the anchor our souls need to always keep us close to God's heart.

Sometimes it's hard to believe that someone could love us so much that they'd forgive us over and over. How

could they keep on loving us as if we had never done anything wrong? But that's exactly how God feels about us. Even when we can't understand why he would love us, we let down our anchors into his promise and trust that he will do everything he says.

I know I am loved because ...

... God's promises are my anchor!

Tongue-Tied

JAMES 1:19–21; 3:2, 4–6

lways be willing to listen and slow to speak. Do not become angry easily. Anger will not help you live a good life as God wants. So put out of your life every evil thing and every kind of wrong you do. Don't be proud but accept God's teaching that is planted in your hearts. This teaching can save your souls....

We all make many mistakes. If there is a person who never said anything wrong, he would be perfect. He would be able to control his whole body, too.... A ship is very big, and it is pushed by strong winds. But a very small rudder controls that big ship. The man who controls the rudder

decides where the ship will go. The ship goes where the man wants. It is the same with the tongue. It is a small part of the body, but it brags about doing great things.

A big forest fire can be started with only a little flame. And the tongue is like a fire. It is a whole world of evil among the parts of our bodies. The tongue spreads its evil through the whole body. It starts a fire that influences all of life. The tongue gets this fire from hell.

291

Royal Connections

Sometimes it seems like we just can't help it. Before we even know it, we've opened our mouths and said words that were hurtful or disrespectful, or complaining. One minute we love Jesus and tell him so, and the next minute we're talking badly to our parents or misbehaving.

God says we shouldn't be this way. He warns us that our tongues can really get us into trouble. We have to work hard

to keep them under control. We need to remember to be quiet when we need to and speak up when we should. Ask God to help you know the difference.

I know I am loved when...

...God helps me be respectful and say nice things.

Prayer Partners

I f one of you is having troubles, he should pray. If one of you is happy, he should sing praises. If one of you is sick, he should call the church's elders. The elders should pour oil on him in the name of the Lord and pray for him. And the prayer that is said with faith will make the sick person well. The Lord will heal him. And if he has sinned, God will forgive him. Confess your sins to each other and pray for each other. Do this so that God can heal you. When a good man prays, great things happen. Elijah was a man just like us. He prayed that it would not rain. And it didn't rain on the land for three and a half years! Then Elijah prayed again. And the rain came down from the sky, and the land grew crops again.

Want to know what real friendship looks like? Read James 5:16. God gives us other Christians in our lives for a reason. God wants to give us blessing through our friends.

We need to be honest with each other, especially those we trust. If you do something wrong, tell it to someone you trust, and they can pray for you. Then maybe you can pray for your friend or parent to help them stay close to God,

too. When we depend upon each other to help us be close to God, our friendships grow deep and strong — not only with each other, but with God, too.

I know I am loved when...

...friends pray for me!

True Beauty

1 PETER 2:20-21, 23-25; 3:3-5

f you suffer for doing good, and you are patient, then that pleases God. That is what you were called to do. Christ suffered for you. He gave you an example to follow. So you should do as he did....

People insulted Christ, but he did not insult them in return. Christ suffered, but he did not threaten. He let God take care of him. God is the One who judges rightly. Christ carried our sins in his body on the cross. He did this so that we would stop living for sin and start living for what is right. And we are healed because of his wounds. You were like sheep that went the wrong way. But now you have come back to the Shepherd and Overseer of your souls....

It is not fancy hair, gold jewelry, or fine clothes that should make you beautiful. No, your beauty should come from within you— the beauty of a gentle and quiet spirit. This beauty will never disappear, and it is worth very much to God. It was the same with the holy women who lived long ago and followed God. They made themselves beautiful in this way.

LIVIN' THE PRINCESS LIFE

Did you know that every group of people around the world has their own ideas about what a beautiful person looks like? Some think being skinny is beautiful. Some think big muscles are cool. And others think larger, rounder bodies are beautiful.

So what is beautiful? To God, real beauty is the way you look on the inside. He sees the person who loves him and wants to obey as someone much more beautiful than the most famous celebrity. A gentle and quiet spirit might not make the headline news here on earth, but it is a cause for celebration in heaven. So don't worry about what you see in the mirror. Instead, ask God to show you what's in your heart. Ask him to make you into a beautiful child of God.

I know I am loved . . .

. . . and that because I love God, too, he makes me beautiful.

Reflecting Light

Dear friends, we should love each other, because love comes from God. The person who loves has become God's child and knows God. Whoever does not love does not know God, because God is love. This is how God showed his love to us: He sent his only Son into the world to give us life through him. True love is God's love for us, not our love for God. God sent his Son to die in our place to take away our sins.

That is how much God loved us, dear friends! So we also must love each other. No one has ever seen God. But if we love each other, God lives in us. If we love each

other, God's love has reached its goal. It is made perfect in us....

We love because God first loved us. If someone says, "I love God," but hates his brother, he is a liar. He can see his brother, but he hates him. So he cannot love God, whom he has never seen. And God gave us this command: Whoever loves God must also love his brother.

LIVIN' THE PRINCESS LIFE

She's sitting all alone. She always does. No one in the class likes her because she dresses differently. Her face is a little strange, too. Some kids don't want to be around her. What should you do?

God says that if we really love him then we should show love to others. If we don't love others, it shows that we don't have the love of God in us. Because God himself is love, he wants us to be like a mirror.

We can reflect his rays of love into other people's lives. Every single person alive is important. Each was made in God's own image. Each person brings glory to God. When we choose to show love to others, we are doing what God created us to do.

I know I am loved ...

... by the way God's love shines through me!

Our Safety Net

Dear friends, remember what the apostles of our Lord Jesus Christ said before. They said to you, "In the last times there will be people who laugh about God. They will do only what they want to do–things that are against God." These are the people who divide you. They do only what their sinful selves want. They do not have the Spirit.

But dear friends, use your most holy faith to build yourselves up strong. Pray with the Holy Spirit. Keep yourselves in God's love. Wait for the Lord Jesus Christ with his mercy to give you life forever.

Show mercy to people who have doubts. Save them. Take them out of the fire. Show

mercy mixed with fear to others. Hate even their clothes which are dirty from sin.

God is strong and can help you not to fall. He can bring you before his glory without any wrong in you and give you great joy. He is the only God. He is the One who saves us. To him be glory, greatness, power, and authority through Jesus Christ our Lord for all time past, now, and forever. Amen.

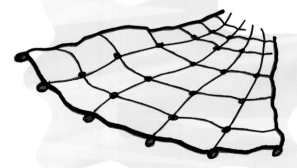

LIVIN' THE PRINCESS LIFE

By this point, you're getting near the end of your new storybook Bible. Lots and lots of Bible words and stories have encouraged you to trust God and live the life he wants for you. It's a lot to remember—but you can read it again and again.

God's way is so different from the way we naturally think and act. You might think it's just impossible to learn and live all you've read. But he hasn't asked you to do something you can't do. Want to know why? Because, in

Jude 24, God promises that he will keep you from falling. He alone can make you into the person you were meant to be. So rejoice! And keep your eyes on your Father who will make you perfect, amazing, and loved!

I know I am loved because . . .
. . . God is the one who saves me!

CRAFT: PAPER-MACHE WORLD

⭐ balloon
⭐ newspaper, torn in strips
⭐ blue liquid starch (paste)
⭐ paint and brushes

INSTRUCTIONS

Day 1: Blow up the balloon as large as you can. Tie it shut.
Pour liquid starch in a plastic bowl that has a lid.
Wet the newspaper strips in the liquid starch, and cover the balloon with the strips. When you have the balloon fully covered, set it aside to dry overnight. Put the lid on the bowl of liquid starch to keep it from drying out.

Day 2: Cover the balloon with a second layer of newspaper strips. Let dry overnight.

Day 3: Cover the balloon with a third layer of newspaper strips. Let dry overnight.

Day 4: Paint your world.

Day 5: Hang your world in your room to remind you of our awesome and powerful God.

310

"In the beginning God created the sky and the earth. The earth was empty and had no form. Darkness covered the ocean, and God's Spirit was moving over the water" (Gen. 1:1-2). How awesome to think that God created the Universe out of nothing! In one day God created the day and the night. The next day, the sky...and so on. Today make your own world using a balloon, newspaper, paste, and paint, then marvel at the power God displayed when he created the world.

Recipe: Fruit Salad

- apples
- oranges
- bananas
- strawberries
- pineapple

Or you can use any fruit you have at home.

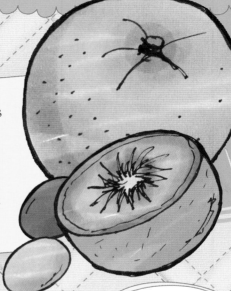

RECIPE

1. Wash and cut the fruit into bite-size pieces.
2. Mix the fruit together in a bowl.
3. Serve it as a snack or a salad for the family dinner meal.

After God created people he said, "Look, I have given you all the plants that have grain for seeds. And I have given you all the trees whose fruits have seeds in them. They will be food for you" (Gen. 1:29). Prepare a fruit salad for your family today, using the foods that God made just for us to eat.

Recipe: Applesauce

INGREDIENTS

- 6 apples
- 1 cup water
- sugar and cinnamon to taste

RECIPE

1. Ask your parent or grandparent to help you peel and cut the apples into chunks.
2. Together, place 12 chunks in the blender with the water and blend.
3. Continue to add the apples until all are blended and soft.
4. Add sugar and cinnamon to taste.

Before you start making your applesauce, ask your parent or grandparent to cut one of the apples in half through the center, dividing the top of the apple from the bottom. When you open the apple halves, you will see two stars inside the apple. In the Bible, God used stars to tell Abraham how many children he would have. He also used a star to lead the wise men to the baby Jesus. The star represents hope and guidance.

There were consequences for Adam and Eve's sin, but God showed them his love even when they sinned. "The Lord God made clothes from animal skins for the man and his wife. And so the Lord dressed them" (Gen. 3:21). When you sin, ask God to forgive you and for his help to resist temptation the next time. Remember the apple and the promise of hope and guidance God hid inside the apple.

CRAFT: GIFT OF LOVE

In presenting their gifts to God, Cain "brought some food from the ground. Abel brought the best parts of his best sheep. The Lord accepted Abel and his gift" (Gen. 4:3-4). Cain gave a gift to God, but Abel gave God his best.

God has gifted you uniquely. There is nobody else like you—never has been, never will be! You may have a talent for singing, writing, making arts and crafts, playing sports, helping friends, or listening. When you do your best in the talents God has given you, it is an act of worship to God. Use the ideas on the next page (or your own) to offer a gift of love to God today.

Ideas for Your Gift of Love

Singing: Sing your favorite song out loud for God to hear.

Writing: Write a love letter to God. Pour out your heart to him in thanksgiving.

Arts and Crafts: Make a creation using your talents to honor God.

Sports: Devote time to practicing and improving your skills to be the best team player you can be for God.

Helping: Find someone who needs help in your family or neighborhood, and thank God for the opportunity to serve them.

Listening: Listen to your friends as they share about their joys and struggles, and pray for them.

Recipe: A Rainbow in the Clouds

INGREDIENTS

- paper plates
- whipped topping (in a can)
- colored cereal loops

RECIPE

1. Squirt out "clouds" of whipped cream onto a paper plate.
2. Next, sprinkle cereal into the whipped cream, or arrange the colored loops into a rainbow shape in the "clouds."
3. Grab a spoon, and enjoy your tasty rainbow treat!

Noah followed God's laws and talked with God, even when everyone around him sinned and did whatever they wanted. Have you ever been in a place where it seemed you were the only one doing what was right? Can you imagine how hard it was for Noah to build an ark in a desert while the people around him laughed at him?

Noah obeyed God, and God saved Noah and his family from the flood. After the flood, God talked to Noah again. He made a promise to Noah: "When I bring clouds over the earth, a rainbow appears in the clouds. Then I will remember my agreement. It is between me and you and every living thing. Flood-waters will never again destroy all life on the earth" (Gen. 9:14-15).

When you feel all alone because you are doing the right thing, remember the story of Noah and the promise God gave him after the flood.

319

Recipe: Sarah's Bread

When Abraham met his guests, he immediately offered them bread to eat and water to wash their feet. Sarah was in the kitchen. Abraham told her to use the best flour and make bread. Making bread or a meal for guests was common in the Bible. Sharing a meal with someone signifies the desire to spend time with them and make them comfortable while they are with you.

Follow the recipe on the next page to make a different kind of dough—playdough! Invite a friend to come over and make the playdough with you, then play with it together, sharing and enjoying each other's company.

INGREDIENTS

- 🌸 1 cup salt
- 🌸 1 cup flour
- 🌸 1 tablespoon vegetable oil
- 🌸 water
- 🌸 food coloring

DOUGH RECIPE

1. Mix the salt and flour together.
2. Add the oil, and mix well.
3. Mix your favorite color of food coloring with the water.
4. Slowly add the colored water a little at a time, until the dough is the right texture.

Recipe: Jacob's Soup

VEGETABLE SOUP INGREDIENTS

- ♡ 1 can corn
- ♡ 1 can sliced carrots
- ♡ 1 can potatoes
- ♡ 2 cans chicken broth
- ♡ 1 can peas or green beans

RECIPE

Open the cans. Pour all the ingredients in a crockpot. Ask your mom to cook the soup on high for 2-3 hours or low for 4-6 hours. Enjoy your hot soup together at dinnertime!

When Esau came home from working in the fields, he was very hungry. Esau was so hungry, in fact, that he let his appetite control his thinking. He let Jacob talk him out of his rights as the firstborn son—all for a bowl of vegetable soup.

Have you ever done something you knew was wrong, but the immediate reward was so tempting, you did it anyway? Maybe you've watched a movie or played a video game you know your parents wouldn't approve, but you watched it anyway. Don't let Satan turn your eyes away from God in a moment of temptation.

After you've finished making your vegetable soup, bring your family together for a great family meal and time of discussion. Talk about some weaknesses you have that sometimes tempt you to give up something God has given you. Help each other to learn how to resist temptation, and ask for God's help.

CRAFT: RAINBOW FILTERS

⭐ Coffee filters

⭐ Spray bottle

⭐ Bold-tip markers

INSTRUCTIONS

1. Using your markers make designs and squiggles on the coffee filters, covering them with ink.

2. When you are done, lay each coffee filter one at a time on 2 paper towels.

3. Squirt the coffee filters with water and watch the markers blend together.

4. Hang your coffee filters to dry with paper towels under them.

5. When you are finished share your rainbows with others and brighten their day!

The first time Joseph is mentioned in the Bible, we are told about the love his father, Jacob, had for him. Jacob showed favoritism to Joseph by making him a special colorful robe. "Joseph's brothers saw that their father loved Joseph more than he loved them. So they hated their brother" (Genesis 37:4).

In life everything is not fair and even. However, as much as possible we need to think about other people's feelings and include them. Today make rainbow filters for your family, friends, and neighbors. Give them away with a smile and let the people around you know how special you think they are.

CRAFT: HEART

God does not expect us

to be perfect, but he does expect us to listen and obey his commands. When God gave the Ten Commandments to Moses, he did not just give us a list of rules. God shared his heart and showed us how he feels when we disobey his Laws. "You must not worship or serve any idol. This is because I, the Lord your God, am a jealous God. A person may sin against me and hate me. I will punish his children.... But I will be kind to thousands who love me and obey my commands" (Exodus 20:5-6).

Did you know that God is jealous? He is. He loves you so much and he wants your praise and attention. The Ten Commandments are more than a list of laws to obey for obedience sake. God gave them to us because he knows that obeying them keeps us from hurting ourselves and others. They are a window into the heart of God and a recipe for us to use to grow closer to him. As you make your heart craft, think about how much God loves you and wants you to know him better.

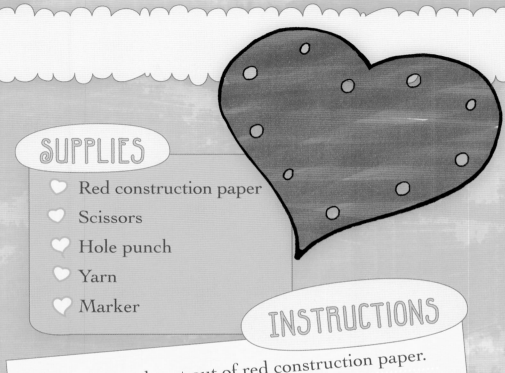

SUPPLIES

- 💛 Red construction paper
- 🤍 Scissors
- 🤍 Hole punch
- 🤍 Yarn
- 💛 Marker

INSTRUCTIONS

1. Cut a large heart out of red construction paper.
2. Punch ten holes evenly spaced around the outer edge of your heart.
3. In the middle of the heart write the Ten Commandments.
4. The ten holes on the outside of the heart represent the Ten Commandments.
5. Lace your heart with yarn connecting the ten holes to form one heart.

327

CRAFT: ANGEL IN THE PATH

Balaam could not see the angel that his donkey saw on the path. Balaam was surprised when he finally saw the angel. How many times have you thought you knew all about a situation only to find out later you did not have all the facts?

God gives us the Bible and our parents to guide us on the path he has set before us. Hang this angel on your closet door to remind you, as you get ready each day, to look to God and your parents for help as you grow in faith and follow him.

- ★ Two-foot square piece of white fabric
- ★ Three-inch Styrofoam ball
- ★ One yard of white string
- ★ Yellow and white pipe cleaners
- ★ Black marker
- ★ Old white tights

INSTRUCTIONS

1. Open your square of fabric and place the Styrofoam ball in the middle.

2. Tie the ball into the middle of the fabric with a 3-foot piece of white string creating the angel's head. Do not cut the string tails off.

3. Cut twelve inches off the bottom of each side of the tights (like creating 2 new socks).

4. Shape your white pipe cleaners in the new "socks" to make wings for the angel.

5. Tie the wings and each end of a yellow pipe cleaner onto the string tails.

6. Shape the yellow pipe cleaner into a halo of your angel.

7. Use the marker to draw a face.

8. Use more string to hang your angel on a closet door hook or over the doorknob.

Recipe: A Hidden Surprise

INGREDIENTS

- Crescent rolls
- Small hotdogs
- Oven

RECIPE

1. Open the package of crescent rolls and unroll them.
2. In each triangle place a small hotdog.
3. "Hide" the hotdogs in the dough and place them on a cookie sheet.
4. Have your parents cook the rolls as directed on the packaging.
5. Enjoy your hidden surprise treat!

Rahab hid the spies under flax plants that were used to make fabric for clothes. God allowed the spies to be hidden to save their lives (see Joshua 2). Later God allowed Rahab and her family also to be hidden to save their lives.

Make the recipe on the previous page for a tasty reminder of God's power to protect and to save us.

CRAFT: BOOKMARK

God made Samson for a special purpose. But Samson did not focus on God. Samson was not going to church, and he did not listen to his God-fearing family and friends. Samson listened to his friend Delilah. Delilah did not believe in God. She did not want the best for Samson. Eventually, Samson told her that his hair was the source of his power. Delilah cut Samson's hair when he was asleep. "In this way she began to make him weak. And Samson's strength left him" (Judges 16:19). We need friends who make us better people and build us up instead of tearing us down.

God makes each of us unique and special. Just like Samson, God has made promises to you. You are important to God and he wants you to be his special child. Make the bookmark on the next page and use it to keep your place as you read God's promises for you in the Bible.

SUPPLIES

- ☐ Construction paper
- ◇ Scissors
- ◇ Markers
- ☐ Stickers
- ◇ School picture
- ☐ Clear packing tape

INSTRUCTIONS

1. Cut a bookmark-sized strip out of construction paper.
2. Decorate the bookmark front and back with markers and stickers.
3. Tape your school picture on the bookmark.
4. Using clear packing tape, seal your bookmark so it will last a long time.

Recipe: Friendship Cookies

- ♥ 2 ¼ c. flour
- ♥ 1 tsp. salt
- ♥ ¾ c. sugar
- ♥ 1 tsp. vanilla
- ♥ 1 ¾ c. chocolate chips
- ♥ 1 tsp. baking soda
- ♥ 2 sticks of butter (softened)
- ♥ ¾ c. packed brown sugar
- ♥ 2 eggs

RECIPE

1. Preheat the oven to 350 degrees.
2. Mix flour, salt, and baking soda and set aside.
3. In another larger bowl mix the butter, eggs, vanilla, and white and brown sugar.
4. While a friend mixes the batter, pour the flour mixture in slowly.
5. Add the chocolate chips last.
6. Drop spoonfuls of dough on ungreased cookie sheets (12 cookies per sheet).
7. Bake one sheet of cookies at a time for 9-11 minutes.

Jonathan and David were best friends. After David killed Goliath, Jonathan's dad had David come to live with them. Jonathan and David formed a close bond and treated each other like brothers.

It is so nice in this world to have friends who care about and look after you. Maybe you already have a friend to share your secrets with. Maybe you're still looking for one such friend. Invite a new or old friend over to make cookies. Give your friend half of the ingredients and take turns following the recipe. When you're done, enjoy your friend and your treat!

CRAFT: SAND CASTLES

SUPPLIES

- Sand
- Squirt bottle with water
- Sand toys

Solomon's wisdom was "as hard to measure as the sand on the seashore" (1 Kings 4:29). God uses sand to describe things that are so big in number we, as humans, cannot understand them. "There were as many people as there were grains of sand on the seashore" (1 Kings 4:20) in Solomon's kingdom.

Yet the God of the universe knows your name, how you feel, and what you desire. How cool is that! Find a sandbox or a plastic tub with sand and have fun building sand castles. Can you count the grains of sand that you are playing with? God can! Think about how big God is and how special you are to him.

CRAFT: GIFT OF SILVER

It was impossible to count Solomon's wealth. Even with all his wealth, people would still travel to bring him more gifts of gold and silver.

The same is true today. God is our King. He created and owns all that is in the world. Yet we still bring him our gifts of money on Sunday to see that his will is done on earth through churches and missionaries.

If you lived in Solomon's day what gift would you bring the king? Using tin foil create a gift for Solomon. You could make a crown, a ring, or a piece to be put in the Temple Solomon built. Have fun and make as many treasures as you wish!

SUPPLIES

- Tin foil

CRAFT: SUGAR CUBE WALL

Before Nehemiah asked the king to let him go rebuild the city walls, he prayed to God. "Lord, listen carefully to my prayer. I am your servant.... Give me, your servant, success today. Allow this king to show kindness to me" (Nehemiah 1:11). When we pray before we do things, we allow God to use us.

Not only did the king allow Nehemiah to rebuild the city walls, but he sent people to help him rebuild them. Before Nehemiah's prayer, the king would not have let the city walls be rebuilt. After his prayer the king went beyond giving permission – to helping rebuild them.

Prayer is powerful. In Joshua's prayer, God tore down the walls of Jericho. In Nehemiah's prayer, God helped to rebuild the walls of Jerusalem.

Think about the walls you want God to tear down or build in your life. As you see your wall this week, pray that God will help you build walls of faithfulness and belief.

SUPPLIES

- 💜 Sugar cubes
- 💜 Glue
- 💜 Food coloring
- 💜 Small paper plate

INSTRUCTIONS

1. On a small paper plate draw a line of glue and place one row of sugar cubes.
2. To make a rainbow wall—use food coloring.
3. Place 1-2 drops of coloring on each sugar cube.
4. Cover the top of the sugar cubes with glue and lay down a second row.
5. Repeat coloring, glue, and sugar cubes until your wall is done.

CRAFT: ESTHER'S CROWN

SUPPLIES

- ⭐ Cereal box
- ⭐ Scissors
- ⭐ Construction paper
- ⭐ Glitter glue
- ⭐ Buttons, sequins, old costume jewelry
- ⭐ Stapler

INSTRUCTIONS

1. Cut a four-inch band off the middle of a cereal box.
2. Cut peaks in the top of the band. Cut and staple the crown to fit your head.
3. Glue construction paper on the crown to cover the cereal label.
4. Decorate your crown with sequins, buttons, glitter glue, and old costume jewelry.

Esther was afraid to talk to the king, but she also knew she might be able to help her family and friends. Esther's cousin Mordecai encouraged Esther when he said, "You might keep quiet at this time. Then someone else will help and save the Jews.... And who knows, you may have been chosen queen for just such a time as this" (Esther 4:14). Mordecai had faith the Jews would be saved. However, he also saw that God had placed Esther in the right place at the right time to help the Jews.

Esther listened to her cousin's advice and was able to be used by God to save the Jews. When you accept Christ as your personal Savior you become a child of God. You too are royalty. You are a princess of the King! Just like Esther, there will be times in your life where you will be in just the right place at just the right time to be used by God to further his kingdom. After you make your crown, put it in your room somewhere where you will see it and remember your relationship to the King of heaven and earth.

Snack: Animal Crackers

SNACK

♡ Animal crackers
♡ Glass of milk

The people wanted Daniel to pray to the king. Daniel knew he should only pray to God. Daniel did what was right even though everyone around him did not. Imagine how scared you would be in the lions' den! Daniel's faith in God was so strong he did not fear the lions.

When Daniel came out of the lions' den the next day the king declared, "God rescues and saves people. God does mighty miracles in heaven and on earth. God saved Daniel from the power of the lions" (Daniel 6:27). The king saw the power of God in Daniel's life.

What lions are you facing today? Do you feel left out? Rejected? Scared? Bullied? Tired? Alone? God knows how you feel and he is here to comfort and protect you. God has given you the Bible to read about how others have felt just like you do. God also has given you your parents, teachers, and leaders to talk to. They will help you learn how to rely on God for everything you need.

Think about the lions in your life and talk to God about them as you enjoy a glass of milk with animal crackers.

MY SPECIAL THOUGHTS